Frederick James Furnivall

The Stacions of Rome and the Pilgrims Sea-Voyage

With Clene Maydenhod

Frederick James Furnivall

The Stacions of Rome and the Pilgrims Sea-Voyage
With Clene Maydenhod

ISBN/EAN: 9783337076030

Printed in Europe, USA, Canada, Australia, Japan

Cover: Foto ©ninafisch / pixelio.de

More available books at **www.hansebooks.com**

The Stacions of Rome,

Pilgrims Sea-Voyage,

and

Clene Maydenhod.

EDINBURGH:	T. G. STEVENSON, 22, SOUTH FREDERICK ST
GLASGOW:	OGLE & CO., 1, ROYAL EXCHANGE SQUARE.
BERLIN:	ASHER & CO., UNTER DEN LINDEN, 20.
NEW YORK:	C. SCRIBNER & CO.
PHILADELPHIA:	J. B. LIPPINCOTT & CO.
BOSTON:	DUTTON & CO.

The
Stacions of Rome,

(In Verse from the Vernon MS., ab. 1370 A.D., and in Prose from the
Porkington MS. No. 10, ab. 1460-70 A.D.,)

and the

Pilgrims Sea-Voyage:

(From the Trin. Coll., Cambridge, MS. R, 3, 19, t. Hen. VI.)

with

Clene Maydenhod.

(From the Vernon MS., ab. 1370 A.D., in the Bodleian Library, Oxford.)

A SUPPLEMENT TO "POLITICAL, RELIGIOUS, AND LOVE POEMS,"
AND "HALI MEIDENHAD,"
(Early English Text Society, 1866.)

EDITED BY

FREDERICK J. FURNIVALL, M.A.,

TRIN. HALL, CAMBRIDGE.

LONDON:

PUBLISHED FOR THE EARLY ENGLISH TEXT SOCIETY,
BY N. TRÜBNER & CO., 60, PATERNOSTER ROW.

MDCCCLXVII.

The
Stacions of Rome,

(In Verse from the Vernon MS., ab. 1370 A.D., *and in Prose from the Porkington MS. No.* 10, *ab.* 1460-70 A.D.,)

and the

Pilgrims Sea-Voyage.

(From the Trin. Coll., Cambridge, MS. R, 3, 19, t. Hen. VI.)

A SUPPLEMENT TO "POLITICAL, RELIGIOUS, AND
LOVE POEMS,"

(Early English Text Society, 1866.)

EDITED BY

FREDERICK J. FURNIVALL, M.A.,

TRIN. HALL, CAMBRIDGE.

LONDON:

PUBLISHED FOR THE EARLY ENGLISH TEXT SOCIETY,
BY N. TRÜBNER & CO., 60, PATERNOSTER ROW.

MDCCCLXVII.

PREFACE.

The Catalogue that Mr Halliwell printed of the contents of the Vernon MS. was, unluckily, one of his own making, and not a copy of that prefixed to the magnificent Southern-dialect volume by the Scribe who wrote it, and which will, I hope, be printed in the next Text that the Society issues from this MS. One result of the non-publication of it before, was, that when searching for other copies of the *Stacyons of Rome*, for the volume of "Political, Religious, and Love Poems," edited by me in the early part of this year for the Society, I saw nothing like the *Stacyons* in the printed Catalogue, and felt sure that the Poem was not in the Vernon MS., notwithstanding Mr Halliwell's warning that his notices "must be accepted as very imperfect." But as there were two entries in that gentleman's Catalogue of "117, *Short Religious Poems*, f. 298, r⁰ β. ; 128, *Short Religious Poems*, fol. 319, r⁰ a," and I had long contemplated continuing the small instalment of these pieces edited by me for the Philological Society (Trans. Pt. II., 1858), I commissioned our Oxford copier to transcribe from the MS. the first and last lines, and burdens if any, of all these Short Poems. The execution of the order was delayed for some months, but when it was completed, and I was turning over the leaves of the copy, what should appear on three of the foolscap sheets, for fol. 314, r⁰ γ, to fol. 315 r⁰ γ, of the MS., but the first and last lines of the different paragraphs of the *Stations*,— thus explaining Mr Halliwell's entry, "Short Religious Poems." A longish piece, evidently A Dialogue between the Virgin and the

Cross of Christ, followed, treated in the same way. What was to be done ? Nothing but groan, say " mistakes are natural to man " (I know they are to me), and print the earlier text. Here accordingly it is, and printed with all its metrical points, and guard-stops on each side of figures and single letters, as in the MS., for an experiment how Members like these points and stops reproduced.

This early Vernon version has not several passages which later transcribers have introduced into the Cotton and Lambeth MSS. It shows that the Lambeth continuation of the Cotton MS. was not a late addition, but that the Cotton had lost its tail. It shows the Lambeth text to be more like it than the Cotton, in the passages which all three contain ; and though it does not clear up any of the puzzles of the later copies, it is interesting, as well for its earlier language as for the new Churches it mentions. These are eleven in number,

St Anthony's, l. 473
St Martin's in the Mount, l. 563
St Marcelle's, l. 609
St Grisogon's, l. 680
St Tyre and St John's, l. 681
St Angelo's, l. 693

St Adrian's, l. 701
St Clement's, l. 704
St Stephen's, l. 705
The Virgin's Chapel, where Thomas à Becket kept school, l. 717
St Urban's, l. 720

and on them Mr William M. Rossetti has, as on those of the former volume, kindly added notes, which follow this Preface. Thus far I had written when I learnt from Sir F. Madden's Appendix to his Preface to his *Syr Gawayne* that (the late) Mr Ormsby Gore's Porkington MS. No. 10, contained a copy of the *Stations* in prose, beginning "In Rome bethe ii° paresche churchs." I at once applied for leave to see the MS., and the present Mr Ormsby Gore forthwith obtained it for me from his mother. Its *Stacyons* proved to be a short and incomplete abstract of our long Poem, in 7½ pages of a very small MS., wisely wound up with an *Et C.*, and I have therefore printed it here for completeness and contrast sake.

The allusion to the sea-voyage to the Holy Land in the *Stations*,

ʒif men wuste . grete and smale
þe pardoun þat is . at grete Rome.

þei wolde tellen . In heore dome.

Hit were no neod . to mon in cristiante

To passe in to þe holy lond . ouer þo sée.

To Jerusalem . ne to kateryne.

has induced me to add to this Text the most amusing Poem on "The Pilgrims' Sea-Voyage and Sea-Sickness," from MS. Trin. Coll., Camb., R. 3, 19, first printed by Mr Halliwell in *Reliquiæ Antiquæ*, vol. 1, p. 2, 3, and to which the present Keeper of the Printed Books in the British Museum, Mr Thomas Watts—encyclopædic in knowledge and gracious in speech—called my attention some twenty years ago. Mr Aldis Wright has himself read the transcript with the MS., and I do not think that any readers will regret its reproduction here.

The cause of *Clene Maydenhod* appearing in this Text is Mr Cockayne's edition of that most vivid sketch of an English girl's temptations to forsake marriage and maternity in 1220 A.D., '*Hali Meidenhad.* It is long since I have been so interested in any treatise ; and seeing that *Clene Maydenhod* was in the Vernon, I could not resist the temptation of printing it, for illustration and contrast sake. The texts are paged separately, so that they may be bound, if wished, with those that they refer to ; and for the same reason the Index to the names of Men and Churches in *Stations* refers to the Cotton and Lambeth versions printed in " Political, Religious, and Love Poems," 1866. Mr George Parker, of Rose Hill, Oxford, has read both the Vernon texts with the MS., and my thanks are due to him for his care.

3, St George's Square, N.W.,
    Dec., 1866.

P.S.—The reviewer in *The Saturday Review* of Dec. 22, 1866, does not understand in what sense we publish our Texts. We print them mainly for our Members ; but, remembering the times when we wanted single volumes of the books of the Camden and Percy Societies, the Abbotsford, Bannatyne and other Clubs, and could not get them, we resolved, when starting the Society, to sell each of our texts separately to any person wanting it, at the publisher's profit on its cost : this—though it would be a great nuisance to us by spoiling our sets—to benefit some poor students who might need help. We sell, perhaps, an average of five copies of each Text separately, against 400 odd issued to Members. This is why I conceive myself entitled to write Prefaces as to a circle of my friends; for such I look on Subscribers as being. Did I consider a Saturday Reviewer and the public as part of my audience, I should certainly write in a different tone to them. To the Saturday man I should say, that the libertinism* of his comments was often unworthy of a Free man ;

---

* This called forth the following remarks—reprinted with the heading, " *The Saturday's* Insolence and *The Saturday's* Ignorance "—from one of our literary journals now discontinued : "Last Saturday's *Punch* contains the following paragraph (p. 35, col. 2, No. 349) :—' Some fiddler advertises himself in the *Musical World* as ' Paganini Redividus.' One would not notice his blunder but for his cheek.' That is our own feeling about a ludicrous blunder occurring in a review of Dr Kingsley's ' Thynne on Chaucer,' in the *Saturday Review* of the week before, written in that tone of ungentlemanlike assumption and petulant insolence for which one writer, at least, in that journal has long been notorious, and which, at a certain period of its existence, drove men like Professor Pearson and Mr Bowen from its columns. Dr Kingsley—evidently not a careful corrector of the press— passed over his printer's error of printing the Anglo-Saxon thorn, or sharp *th*, þ, as *r*, ɼ. For this he was jeered at by his reviewer in the regular vulgar-little-boy fashion ; and then, by way of displaying his own learning, the little boy went on to explain the difference between *th* and *r*. But as strutting daws unwittingly drop the peacock's feathers out of their tails, so this unlucky boy either did not know, or did not notice, that he or his printer had put an Anglo-Saxon *w* (ɼ) for the *th* (þ) ; so that there, while he (the clever reviewer) was pointing at Dr Kingsley for his ignorance or carelessness, he was all the time displaying his own, and deliberately forcing every one's attention to the display. Scholars at the Museum, Bodleian, Cambridge, Lambeth, and elsewhere, have enjoyed the self-inflicted punishment that the reviewer's nasty-tempered notice of a book by a courteous, well-read, and widely-esteemed gentleman and man of letters has met with. We make it public on *Punch's* principle—' One would not notice his blunder but for his cheek ; '— but we trust we shall have no more such exhibitions in the *Saturday's* pages ; and for the benefit of the reviewer we reprint for him the judgment he passed on his better,—commending to him the study of his ' Anglo-Saxon Grammar,' the ' Printer's Guide,' and ' *The Book of Courtesy.*'—Of course, we shall be told that all these things are trifles [one ' thing ' was the putting a comma for a full stop], most likely misprints. We answer that accuracy and inaccuracy are not trifles, and that a [writer] of a philological [review], who is either so ignorant that he cannot read his text, or so careless that he lets pass misprints which turn that text into nonsense, displays exactly the same *crassa ignorantia* as an architect who can do everything except build a house, or a surgeon who can do everything except cut off a leg." — *The Reader*, Feb. 3, 1866. What wonder that this man calls my masterly

that wandering through Summer Meads he should be greeted in eye and ear by sights and sounds that should bring him into sweet accord with them, and prevent his always printing every "nasty-tempered" thing he can lay tongue on ; that instead of leaving a set of men—of whom the chief workers are all poorer than himself—to do a work of much help to him, without his help, but with his sneers, it would be more like a generous gentleman to send his subscription to the Society, and print a text for it with his *Saturday* pay. I should ask of the chief Cook who presides over the making of the weekly pudding that tickles so many palates and disturbs so many inwards, that he should pick out the bits of grit in the dab of pabulum contributed to his seventh-day compound by the reviewer I have been addressing. To the public on the other hand I should say, what a very stupid public it is for not supporting more vigorously the best and most liberal Early English printing Society that has ever existed: that there are several thousand well-to-do men in this country who can easily spare a guinea a year each to make their forefathers' speech and thoughts better known to this and future generations ; and they ought so to spare it. To the Historian and Antiquary the Society's work yields rich fruit ; to the Tory who glories in the past, it appeals with strongest claim ; to the Liberal who pleads, as cause for modern justice, the ancient tale of poor men's wrongs that starts before the Conquest, the Society makes heard the voice he listens for. Every man of culture is bound to support us ; and yet hardly any do. The Sanskrit Text Society starts—most rightly—with a first year's subscription of over £1200. The Early English Text Society with a miserable £152. In its third year its income is not much over £600 ; and when it asks for money to print nineteen Texts in one year, it hardly gets money for eleven. The apathy of English lettered men on this subject is a disgrace to them ; and a journal like *The Saturday*, which has a chance of rousing them from it, would be much better employed in

.

strokes of irony (N.B.), nonsense, and my brilliant satire (N.M.), bad jokes ? When you hear a little boy on Hampstead Heath call to a known cross-country rider, " Why don't you get inside ? " need you ask whether the ingenuous youth is a judge of a seat, or is—a little boy ?

doing so than in picking out little blemishes in the Society's Texts, and holding them up to show off a reviewer's fancied cleverness, which, as has been shown in some instances, and can be shown in others, has often turned out to be ludicrous ignorance. If we (as we do) point out some of our own shortcomings, we are thankful enough to have others shown us in the right spirit and the right way. The wrong in both,* I for one will protest against as best I can.

F. J. F.

* The later review of Mr Perry's edition of Hampole's *Short Prose Treatises* is written in the right and gentleman-like spirit.

NOTES ON THE STACIONS OF ROME,

By W. M. ROSSETTI.

The notes which I wrote to the previous publication of the Early English Text Society, the "Stacyons of Rome" printed from the Cotton and Lambeth MSS., apply in great part to the present earlier version of the same poem from the Vernon MS. There are, however, considerable differences of detail between the MSS., of most of which I must leave the reader to take count for himself; and some churches, not named at all in the previously published version, are mentioned in the one now printed. On these churches, and on another point or two here and there, I proceed to offer a few notes upon the same plan as in the former instance.

Line 40. I must take this opportunity to rectify a slip of the pen in my notes upon the Cotton MS. copy, at the corresponding line, No. 56. The altar mentioned in that line is to "Seynt Symon," or, in the Lambeth and the present Vernon MSS., to "Seint Symon & Jude;" I made the slip of saying that the Cotton MS. specified an altar "to St Jude."

Lines 55-6. The statement here made is that St Peter's Basilica was consecrated "Of Seint Martin þat ciȝtcþe day." In the Cotton MS., lines 121-2, this same statement is made concerning the Basilica of San Paolo fuori le Mura; and St Peter's is stated on the contrary to have been consecrated "On Seynt Petur & Powle day." It appears that the Vernon MS. is correct, and that the two statements made in the Cotton MS. ought to be inverted.

Line 118. *Scala Cœli.* Compare this from "God speed the Plough,"

Then commeth prestis that goth to rome.
For to haue siluer to singe at Scala celi.
Lansdowne MS., 762, *fol.* 6.

Line 126. "In tyme of *Tibian* þe Emperour." This potentate, unrecorded by historians, in whose reign 10,000 martyrs suffered in Rome, may perhaps be conjectured to be nominally compounded out of Tiberius, Trajan, and Julian—

a very Cerberus of tyranny, persecution, and apostasy. The Cotton MS. limits itself to the first of these three, " Tyberye "—whose reign was assuredly free from any such wholesale persecution.

Line 160. The " holy bones " here named are to be understood as the bones of Sts Peter and Paul. As I pointed out in my former notes, neither the Cotton MS. in saying that these bones lay undiscovered 500 years, nor yet the Vernon MS. in assigning 100 years as the period, can be trusted : the true time being probably more like 19 months.

Lines 183-4 speak of 44 martyr popes who " liueden " in a chapel in the catacombs ; in the Cotton MS. it is 46 martyr popes who " lyene " there.   I presume that " lyene " is the correct word—if indeed any item of so preposterous an assertion can be termed correct.

Lines 333-4 speak of

> " þe cloþ þat crist was wounden Inne
> Whon he was child for monnes sinne ; "

which seems to mean the swaddling-clothes of the Nativity. These lines correspond to 426-7 in the Cotton MS.,

> " And þe cloþis þat criste was wonden In
> When he shulde dye for mannis syn " ;

this latter statement appears to be the more correct, the actual object in question being the face-cloth.

Lines 357-8. According to the position of these lines in the context, the heads of Sts Peter and Paul were under the high altar in the Chapel Sancta Sanctorum in the old Lateran Palace of the Popes. It may be inferred that the lines have slipped a little out of their proper place ; and that the high altar really spoken of is that of the Basilica of St John Lateran, which would make the statement about the heads correct. These heads were discovered in or about 1365, in the reign of Pope Urban V., which commenced in 1362. The date of the Vernon MS. is about 1370, when the discovery must still have been an interesting novelty to actual or intending pilgrims to Rome: and, in accordance with this date, we find that the lines of the Cotton MS., 456-9,

> "There ys no man now y-bore," &c.,

which my previous notes cited for the purpose of fixing the date of that MS. at not later than 1445, do not appear at all in the Vernon version of the poem.

Line 427. The Church here (and also in the Lambeth MS.) named " of Seynt veuian " (Vivian) is termed "of Julyan " in the Cotton MS.   I am not aware that any Church of St Vivian exists in Rome.

Line 437. St Eusebius is here introduced as connected with the aforenamed Church of St Vivian. The Lambeth MS., however, line 554, speaks of the Church of St Eusebius himself, which I presume to be correct ; but the poem hereabouts in all the three MSS. is obviously a good deal muddled. Compare l. 442 Vernon with l. 559 Lambeth.

Lines 463-4 are new in the Vernon MS. My old authority, Franciuo, confirms the statement that a (daily) indulgence of 1000 years and Lents is to be obtained at St Matthew's Church—to which he adds the remission of one-seventh of one's sins.

Lines 473-4. *The Church of St Anthony* is named in the Vernon MS. only, l. 473 having evidently slipped out of the Lambeth MS. by mischance. There are in Rome two Churches of St Anthony;—one near Sᵃ Maria Maggiore and St Praxed's, with a Hospital; the other named Sant' Antonio de' Portoghesi, near La Scrofa, dedicated by Pope Gelasius to Sts Anthony and Vincent. To it are annexed a hospital for the Portuguese, and many indulgences and privileges for that nation. The particular grace mentioned by our poet, the remission of one-seventh of one's penance, is not, however, confirmed by Francino with regard to either of these churches.

Lines 529 to 532 set forth the indulgences attaching to Sᵃ Maria Maggiore from Assumption-day to the feast of the Virgin's Nativity (15 August to 8 September). The Lambeth MS. says, Assumption-day to Christmas-day, which is an error.

Line 536. Here the name "Prudencian" is erroneous; it should be, as in the Lambeth MS., "Pudencyam"—St Pudentiana.

Line 548. The Vernon MS. reads "hostelled," instead of "harborowed," as in the Lambeth MS.; confirming the inference in my former notes that the statement applies "rather to the house of Pudens than to the cemetery."

Line 558. The extraordinary term "Emperour seint Antonine" seems to point to some corruption of the text. As observed in the former notes, the incident referred to could not, by comparison of dates, have happened in the reign of any of the Antonines.

Lines 563 to 568. *The Church of San Martino in Monte, called also San Silvestro e San Martino,* was built by Symmachus I. in A.D. 500, on the Esquiline Hill, upon the ruins of the Thermæ of Trajan, and was modernized in 1650. There had been an earlier church on the same spot, founded by S. Silvester in the time of Constantine. I know of no particular reason why the text should specify that the edifice " is not round." The text states that Popes Silvester and Leo are buried under the high altar. I do not find Leo named elsewhere; Murray's Handbook mentions Silvester and Martin I., and Francino concurs in this statement, adding the names of three other Popes.

Lines 569 to 572. There is a Church of San Salvatore del Lauro which stands on the site of the laurel-grove near the Portico of Europa. It was founded in 1450, nearly a century later than the date of our Vernon MS., so that one cannot refer to this Church the allusion in the text. This is the only Church " of seint Saluator " known to me in Rome.

Line 601. Our present text seems to be correct in here naming " Seint Sabyne " (Sabinus), instead of the " Seint Sabasabyne " of the Lambeth MS.

Lines 609 to 612. *The Church of St Marcellus,* in the Corso, was built by a Roman lady in the 4th century, in honour of Pope St Marcellus, who, by order of Maxentius, was confined in this spot over a stable, the stench of which is alleged to have killed him. It was rebuilt in 1519 by Sansovino, the façade being of a later date. The ceremony of the Exaltation of the

Cross is held here on 14 September. Francino does not specify the 1000 years' indulgence of our text, but plenary remission on St Marcellus's day.

Lines 655-6 state that the good knight sometime named Placidas lies at the Church of St Eustace. In the Lambeth MS. the person thus named is St Eustace himself; and, as I can find out nothing about Placidas, I am disposed to infer that he and Eustace are one and the same person.

Line 664 clears up the difficulty in the corresponding line, 866, of the Lambeth MS., which states that "the Mawdlene" is in the Church of St Cecilia. We now learn that this is a foot of the Magdalene.

Line 680. *The Church of San Grisogono* (Chrysogonus), a saint who was martyred at Aquileia under Diocletian, is in the Trastevere, and supposed to date originally from the time of Constantine; rebuildings took place in 1129 and 1623. An Englishman may like to remember this church in connection with Archbishop Langton, who was its titular Cardinal. The 400 years' indulgence of our poem is not confirmed by Francino, but plenary remission on the day of St Chrysogonus.

Lines 681 to 688. I cannot clearly identify the "chirche of seint tyre and seint Ion;" but should suppose it to be not improbably *the Church of Sts John and Paul.* There are at least six other churches in Rome bearing the name of St John. The Church of Sts John and Paul—not the apostles, but martyrs of the reign of Julian—was built on the Cœlian Hill, in the 4th century, on the site of the house of these Saints.

Lines 693 to 696. "Seint Angel" may be either *the Church of Sant' Angelo in Borgo,* or that of Sant' Angelo in Pescaria, close to the Portico of Octavius, and interesting in connection with the enterprise of Rienzi. I should rather suppose it to be the former church, which was built by a beatified Pope Gregory in consequence of his having seen the Archangel Michael sheathing his blood-stained sword above the citadel, or Mole of Hadrian. Francino does not name 1000 years' indulgence as applicable to either of these churches; but plenary remission, at the first, on the octave of St Michael, and, at the second, on the 18th July and 29th September.

Line 701. *The Church of St Adrian* is in the Forum, and is said to be the ancient Ærarium consecrated to this Saint by Pope Honorius.

Line 704. *The Church of St Clement,* between the Colosseum and the Lateran, is built over a still more ancient church, which was discovered in 1858, with results of great importance to Christian archæology; the upper church dates probably from the beginning of the 12th century. The traditional origin of the whole foundation was an oratory built by Clement the third Bishop of Rome, a fellow-labourer with St Paul. Instead of the 2000 years' indulgence of the text, Francino specifies plenary remission on the Monday following the second Sunday of Lent, as well as a daily indulgence of 40 years and Lents, doubled during Lent.

Line 705. The Church of "seint Steuene" is probably the Church of *santo stefano Rotondo,* on the Cœlian Hill, now generally supposed to have been originally the circular portion of the Macellum Grande, or Butchers'-

meat Market, erected in Nero's time. It was consecrated by Simplicius I. in A.D. 467, and restored by Nicholas V. towards 1447. Rome contains at least two other churches to St Stephen.

Lines 707 to 712 revert to the Church of " seint saluatour " ; see l. 569. The " Bethleem " here mentioned is, 1 suppose, a Chapel of the Nativity.

Lines 717 to 719. I have been unable to trace the " *Chapel of vre ladi* " at which St Thomas of Canterbury kept school. It may be a separate building; or it may possibly be merely a chapel in the church last previously mentioned, that of St Alexius, which does, it seems, contain (as Francino relates it) " that image of the most blessed Virgin, on the high tabernacle, which used to be in the city of Edessa—before which the most blessed Alexius, being in the said city, often made prayer. And, going one day to the said church to pray, he found the doors closed; and the said image said twice to the porter, ' Open and give entrance to the Man of God, Alexius, who is worthy of heaven.' "

Lines 720 to 726. *The Church of St Urban*, here mentioned, does not appear in my authorities.

The last service I can tender for my reader's acceptance may be to refer him to a book bearing very closely upon the subject-matter of the " Stacions of Rome," and which I find thus entered in a Bookseller's catalogue :— " Mirabilia Romæ ; a German Block-book of nearly 200 pages, being a Handbook for the Pilgrims at Rome in the 15th century. With the most curious descriptions of the relics kept in the Churches ; among them the head of St Peter, milk of the Virgin, the circumcisions of Christ, &c.—and of the indulgences given by the priests of the various Churches. Small 4to ; 12 copies only reprinted in facsimile by J. Ph. Berjeau." One regrets to read this last item, suggesting the small number of people that will ever be able to benefit by the reprint of so curious a book.

W. M. ROSSETTI.

P.S.—On the Porkington MS. I observe :

1. S. Sylvester in 1303, in connection with the heads of Peter and Paul, is a blunder.

2. S. Benyan's Church near S. Gellyan's. This Benyan is Julian in one MS. and Vivian in another : of Benyan I know nothing, but investigation might *possibly* bring something to light.

3. Placidas, the same person as Eustace : so I had guessed in writing on the Vernon MS. ; and that conjecture may now be put positively.

The Stacions of Rome.

[Vernon MS., fol. 314, col. 3. The metrical points, and stops on each side of figures and after single letters, are those of the MS. Hyphens are put in by the Editor. The lines in the foot-notes refer to those of the Stacyons in *Political, Religious, & Love Poems*, pp. 113-44, E.E.T.Soc. 1866. C. stands for Cotton MS., Caligula A ii: L. for Lambeth MS. 306. This Vernon poem has been crossed through with the pen; also two lines have been drawn through the word *pope* in nearly every place where it occurs. The paragraph sign is alternately red and blue.]

Hose wole . his soule leche.

Lustne to me .I. wol him teche

Pardoun . Is þi soule bote.

4 At grete Rome . þer is þe Roote.   *At Rome is the root of Pardon.*

Pardoun . a word in frensch hit is.

Forʒiuenesse . of þi synnes i-wis.

¶ þe Duchesse of troye . þat sum tyme was.

8 To Rome com . wiþ gret pres.

Of hire com Romilous . and Romilon.   *Romilous and Romilon founded Rome.*

Of whom . Rome furst bi-gon.

Heþene hit was . and cristned nouʒt.

12 Til petur . and poul . hit hedde I.-bouʒt.   *Peter and Paul bought it with*

Wiþ Gold . ne seluer . ne wiþ no goode.

Bot wiþ heore flesch . and with heore blode.   *their blood.*

For þei soffrede boþe dede.

16 Heore soule te saue . fro þe quede [1]

---

[1] The Cotton MS. inserts here lines 17-24, which the Lambeth MS. 306 follows the Vernon in omitting.

At *St Peter's*

At seint peter . we schul bi-ginne.

to telle of pardoun . þat slakeþ sinne.

A feir Munstre . men mai þer se.

are 29 steps,

20 Niȝene and twenti greces þer be.

As ofte . as þou gost vp . Or doun.

Bi cause of deuocioun .

at each of which

þou schalt haue . at vche gre .

you get 7 years'
pardon.

24 Mon . or Wommon . wheþer þou be.

Seuene ȝer . to pardoun

And þer-to godes benisoun.

¶ Pope Alisaundre hit graunted at Rome

28 To alle men . þat þider come.[1]

In þat Munstre . men may fynde.

When the 100
Altars are blessed,

An hondred Auteres . bi-foren and be-hynde.

And whon þe Auters .I.-halewed wore.

you get 28 years'
pardon and Lents,

32 xxviij[2] . ȝer . and so mony lentones more.

He ȝaf . and graunted . to pardoun.

And þer-to . godes benysoun.

There are 7 chief
Altars, those of

¶ Among þe Auters . seuene þer be.

36 More of grace . and dignite.

I. the Vernicle,

¶ þe Auter of þe vernicle is on.

Vp-on þe riht hond . as þou schalt gon .

II. Our Lady,

¶ þe secunde . in þe honour of vr ladi is.

III. St Simon
and Jude,
IV. St Andrew,

40 ¶ þe þridde . of seint Symon and Jude I.-wis.

¶ þe Feorþe . of seint Andreuȝ . þou schalt haue

V. St Gregory,

¶ þe Fifþe of seint gregori . þer he lyth in graue

VI. St Leo,

¶ þe Sixte . of seint leon þe pope.

44 þer he song masse . in his Cope.

VII. Holy Cross.

¶ Of seint Crois . þat seuenþe is.

In wȝuche, no wommon schal comen I.-wis.[3]

At St. Peter's
Altar

At þe Auter . þer peter is don.

48 þe pope Gregori . ȝaf gret pardon.

---

[1] l. 37-44 inserted.   [2] xxiiij Cotton MS., xviij Lambeth.

[3] l. 63-6 inserted.

Of sunnes forȝeten . and oþes also.

xxviij . ȝer . he ȝaf þer to.

From holy þursday . In to lammasse

52 Eueriche day . more and lasse.

¶ þenne is xiiij þousend ȝer.

To alle þat come . to þat Munster.

Of seint Martin . þat eiȝteþe day.[1]

56 þat Munstre was halwed . as I.ou say.

þenne is xiiijM ȝer . and lentones þer-to.

þe þridde part . of þi penaunce vndo.

Whon þe vernicle schewed is.

60 Gret pardoun . forsoþe þer is .I.-wis

þreo þousend ȝer . as I. ow telle

To Men þat in . þe Cite dwelle.

And men þat dwelle be sydeward.

64 Nyne þousend ȝer . schal ben heore part.

¶ And þou þat passest ouer þe seé.

Twelue þousend ȝer . is graunted to þe.

And þerto . þow schalt winne more.

68 þe þridde part for-ȝiuenes . of al þi sore.

In lentone is . an holy grace.

Vche pardon is doubled . in þat place.[2]

To seint poul . as I. wene.

72 Foure Myle is . holde bi-twene.

In þat wey . Is gret pardoun.

And of mony sunnes . Remissioun.

Saul was his name . be-foren.

76 Siþen the tyme . þat he was born.

Heþene he was . and cristnet nouȝt.

Til crist put hit . in his þouȝt.

¶ þat holy Mon . Ananias.

80 Him cristnet . þorw godes gras.

And cleped him Poul . petres broþer.

For þe ton schulde . cumforte þe toþer.

Sidenotes (right margin):

Is 28 years' pardon,

and daily from Holy Thursday to Lammas

14,000 years.

On the anniversary of the consecration of the Minster, 14,000 years, &c.

When the Vernicle is showed.

[Fol. 314 b. col. 1.

3000 years to dwellers in the City,

9000 to dwellers near,

12,000 to those who cross the sea.

In Lent all pardons are doubled.

On the road to St Paul's is

great pardon.

(Saul was his name

till Ananias christened him

Paul.)

On St Paul's Con-
version day is 100
years' pardon ;

at his Festival
1000 years.

On Childermas-
day, 4000 years,

and for a whole
year's Sundays

as much pardon
as for a pilgrimage
to St James's.

At *St Anas-
tasius's,*

daily.

7000 years'pardon

Pope Urban

forgives contrite
men all their sins.

Silvester forgives
pilgrims to this
church

broken penance
and oaths.

Outside is the
stone on which
St Paul was
beheaded,

whence 3 wells
prung

that heal the sick.

In þat ilke . conuercioun.

84 He ȝaf an hondred ȝer . to pardoun.

And at þe feste . of his day.

A þousend ȝer . haue þou may.

¶ On childermasse day . In cristemasse

88 Is foure þousend ȝer . to more and lasse.[1]

And ȝif þou beo þere . al þe ȝer.

Vche sunday . in þat munster

þou shalt haue . as muche pardoun.

92 As þou to seint Jame . went and com.

HEr may we . not longe be

To seint Anastace . moste we.

Two Myle . is holde be-twene.

96 Of feir wey . and of grene.

Vche day . ȝif þou wolt craue.

Seuen þousent ȝer . þer may þou haue [2]

Pope Vrban . þat holy syre.

100 So rewardede . men heore huyre

Men þat ben schriuen . and verrey contrit.

Of alle heore synnes . god [3] makeþ heom quit.

¶ Pope Siluestre . to pilgrimes.

104 þat þider comeþ . diuerse tymes.

Penaunce broken . and oþes also.

His oune helpe . he putte þerto.

Wrapþing of Fader . or Moder . ȝif hit be

108 In godes nome . he forȝiueþ þe.[4]

Bi-fore þe dore . stont a ston.

Seynt poules hed . was leyd þeron.

A traitur . smot of his heued.

112 Wiþ a sword . þer hit was leued.

þer aftur spronge welles þre.

Hose is þere . wel may he se.

Of water . boþe feir and gode

116 Men . and Wimmen . han had heore bote

---

[1] l. 121-4 inserted.   [2] l. 135-6 inserted.
[3] Cott. he [Pope Urban]   [4] l. 147-8 inserted.

IN þat place . a Chapel is.
Scala celi . clepet hit is.
Laddere of heuene men clepeþ hitte.

Scala Cœli is
there, Our Lady's
second Chapel.

120 In þe honour of vr ladi . be my witte
þat is þe secounde chapel . of here.
þat men in Roome . tellen þere.
Mony is . þat holy bone.

124 þat vnder þe heiȝe Auter is done.
Ten þousend Martyres . with honour.
In tyme of Tibian[1] . þe Emperour.
þei suffrede deþ . alle in Rome.

10.000 Martyrs
died there in
Tiberian's reign.

128 Heore soules in heuene for to come.
þer men may helpe . quike . and dede
As þe clerkes . in bokes rede[2]
Foure and fourti popes . granted þan.

Prayer there helps
both quick and
dead.

132 þat liggen . at seint Sebastian.
Pope Vrban . Siluestre . and Benet.
Leon . Clement . confermede hit.

Nou passe we forþ . in vre gate

136 To seinte Marie . þe Nunciate
Two Mile is bitwene .I. vnder-stonde.
But þi aren . sumdel longe.
þer is writen . as I. ow say.

To St Mary the
Nunciate's is 2
long miles.

140 Of vre ladi . in þat way.
A-doun heo com wiþ Angeles.
To a Frere of þat hous.
And seide to þat ilke mon.

[Fol. 314 b. col. 2.]
Our Lady
promised to save
from hell-fire
sinners who came
there.

144 þat out of dedly synne . þider com.
Fro þe fuir of helle . heo wolde him schilde.
As heo was Mayden . and moder Mylde[3].

TO Fabian and Bastian . passe we

To St Fabian and
Bastian's is 3
miles.

148 þider we haue . Myles þre
An Angel from heuene . a-doun com.
To seint Gregor . þat holy mon.

An Angel told
St Gregory

---

[1] ? For Tiberian   [2] l. 171-9 inserted.   [3] l. 195-8 inserted.

As he song masse . atte heiȝe Auter.

152 Of seint Sebastian . þat holy Marteer.

And seide here . in þis place.

Is liȝt of heuene . bi godes grace

þer is . of mony sunnes . remissioun

156 And Fourti ȝer . to pardoun

And also monye lentones mo.

Pope Gelasius . ȝaf þer to.

As muche pardoun . is þere.

160 So is . in seint peteres Munstere.

Be þe enchesun . of þe holy bones.

þat þere . weore buried at ones.

And þere lay . [1] vnder grounde

164 An hundred ȝer . er þei weore founde

Afturward . þorw godes grace

þei weore founden . In þat place

And worschuped . with gret Solempnite[2]

168 As þei ouȝte for to be.

OF sixe popes . tellen I.wile[3]

On aftur oþur . as hit is skile.

Pope Pelagius .I. telle þe.

172 Gregor . and Siluester . þer beoþ þre.

Alisaundre . and Nichole . þer beoþ fyue.

Honorius þe sixte . while he was on lyue

Vche of hem . ȝaf his grace.

176 A þousend ȝer . in that place

To alle þat euere . þat þer beone.

And of dedly sunnes be clene.

For elles may þi soule . not lyue.

180 Bot of dedly sunnes . þou be schriue.

---

[1] Cotton MS. inserts 'petur & powle,' and makes the 'an'
next line 'Fyfe.'

[2] This line is omitted in the Cotton MS.

[3] This line is erased by a later hand in the Vernon MS.
puts l. 171 here before l. 169.

A lutel be-hynde . þou maiʒt go.
þer stont a Chapel . in a wro.
Foure and fourti popes . sum time were.
184 verrey Martirs . þat liueden þere.
vche of hem . ʒaf his beuisoun.
For þer is plener remissioun[1].
Of alle þe sunnes . þou hast I.-don.
188 Sin þou in þis world . coom.
Al is . for-ʒeuen þe.
So I . herde of clerkes . þat þer han be.
And ʒif þow dye . þiderward.
192 Heuene blisse . schal ben þi part.
But þou most take . Candel liht[2].
Elles þou gost . Merk as niht[2].
For vnder þe corþe . most þou wende.
196 þow maiʒt not seo . bi-fore ne bi-hynde.
For þider fledde Mony men.
For drede of deþ . to sauen hem.
And suffrede peynes . harde and sore.
200 In heuene to dwelle . for euer more

Nou wende we . to þe palmalle.
domine quo uadis . men hit calle
þer Peter mette with Ihesu.
204 And seide lord . whoder woltou.
Crist onswerde . to peter þo
In to Rome . he seide I. go.
Eft to dye . on Rode for þe
208 þou dredest to dye . peter for me.
Lord he seide . Merci I. crie.
To take my deþ .I. am redie.
þer is a signe . of his foot.
212 On Marbel ston . þer he stod.
Vche day . two þousent ʒer
Of pardoun . þou mai haue þer.

---

[1] C. omits this line.
[2-2] C. transposes and slightly alters these lines.

þer is writen on a ston . gret pardoun
216 þer is of alle sunes . Remissioun[1].

At seint thomas þe Apostel of Inde,

a chirche i-wis . þou mai· þer fynde
put þin hond . wiþ almes dede

220 And þou schalt haue . þer gret mede
To helpe hem . þat ben þere.

In þe holi lond . or elles where.

Niht and day . to preye for þe.

224 For help of þi charite.

Of moni popes . þat þer han bene.

þis pardoun to þe . is graunted clene.
Fourtene þousend ჳer . and sum del more

228 þe þridde part forჳiuenesse . of þi sore.

And pardon in Rome . þat is grete.

þe Stacions . þer men hit clepe

Pope Bonefas . confermed alle.

232 For euer more . lasten hit schalle.

To seint Ion lateran . moste we.

A while þere . for to be.
To telle of pardoun . þat is þore.

236 For in al Rome . ne is no more.

þen þer is graunted . of Ihesu crist.

þorw preyer of seint Ion þe Ewangelist,

And seint Ion Baptist also.

240 To alle . þat þider wol go.
¶ For sum tyme was . an Emperour,

þat liuede in Rome . wiþ gret honour.
Kyng Costantyn . men dude him calle

244 Boþe in boure . and eke in halle.
In Mahoun . was al his þouht.

For in crist . ne leeuede he nouht.
A . Mesel forsoþe . we fynde he was.

248 Til crist sende him . of his gras.

[1] C. l. 268-77 inserted, about St John of the Latin gate.

¶ Pope Siluestre . gon him preche.

Cristes lawes . forte teche.

So leeuede he wel . In godes sone.

252 And cristene mon . wolde he bi-come.

He dude him cristne . as I. ou telle

In þis Miracle . þus hit bi-felle

þat þe water wesch . a-wey his sinne

256 And al þe fulþe . þat he was Inne.

¶ þenne spak þe Emperour. .

To pope siluestre with gret honour.

Siluestre he seide . godes clerke.

260 I. mai seo nou . þat er was derke.

Mi misbileue . haþ blyndet me.

þat I . mihte . þe [soþe¹] not se.

Of godes mihtes . ne of his werkes.

264 I. wol bi-comen . on of his clerkes.

Mi paleys I ȝiue hit . to þin honde.

Of me þou schalt hit vnderfonge

And mak þer-of . godes hous.

268 For I. wole . þat hit beo þous.

I. wol him loue . with al mihtes.

And preic him to ben . on of his knihtes.

And whon þou hast . so I.-do.

272 ȝif þi benyson . þer-to.

To alle hem . þat þider come.

To honoure . godes sone.

And seint Jon . þe Ewangelyst.

276 Peter and poul . and seint Jon þe Baptist.

Pope siluester . þenne seide he.

Of peter and poul . and of me

þei schal be clene . of synne and pyn.

280 As crist clanset . þe of þyn.

And as þe fulþe . fel fro þe.

So clene of sunne . schal þei be.

¹ C. inserts *mote*, and L. *soothe*.

Right margin glosses:

till Pope Silvester

converted and

christened him.

The water washed away his sins and disease,

and he

acknowledged

his misbelief,

gave up his palace to be

God's House,

and asked Silvester to bless all worshippers there.

Silvester promised them

cleansing from
all sin.
Of alle maner clansyng of synne.

284 þat non schal dwellen . heore soule with-inne

¶ Pope Bonefas . telleþ þis tale .

If men did but
know the
pardon to be had
at Rome,
[1] ʒif men wuste . grete and smale

þo pardoun þat is . at grete Rome.

288 þei wolde tellen . In heore dome.[1]

they'd not go
Hit were no neod . to mon in cristiante

to the Holy
Land or St
Catherine's;
To passe in to þe holy lond . ouer þe séé.[2]

To Jerusalem . ne to kateryne.

292 To bringe monnes soule . out of pyne

for in Rome is
pardon without
end; and
For pardoun þer is . with-outen ende.

Wel is him . þat þider may wende [3]

Relics too—
Rerikes þer beo . monyon

296 In worschupe of crist . and seynt Ion.

· In þe Rof . ouer þe popes se.

I. A Saviour, not
painted by man;
A saluatour . þer may þou se

Neuer I.-peynted . with hond of Mon.

300 As men I. Roome . tellen con.

[Fol. 315, col. 1.]
Whon Seluestre halwed þat place.

Hit apeered þer . þorw godes grace.

¶ [4] Anoþer chapel is . in þat hous.

304 þer-Inne beoþ Relikes . precious.[4]

II. The Table of
the Last Supper;
þe Table . þer men may se.

þat crist made . on his maunde

On scherþorsday . whon he brak bred.

308 Bi-fore þe tyme . þat he was ded.

Eteþ of þis . hit doþ ʒow good.

Hit is my flesch . and my blod.

Whon ʒe schul me . here not fynde.

312 Hit schal ʒou kepen . from þe feende.

[1-1] For these three lines C. has one, l. 349, 'And y tell ythe
forth with-outene fayle.'

[2] See the poem at the end of this about the miseries of the
Pilgrim's sea-sickness.

[3] l. 356-71 inserted.

[4-4] Omitted by C., see l. 380: L. has them.

¶ ¹ A-bouen an Auter . is maked of tre.

Is a table I. telle þe

Vnder þat auter . In a whucche is done.   III. In a hutch

316   Wiþ holy Relikes . monione.¹

- ¶ Two tables þer is .I. vnderstonde.   the Two Tables of the Law given

þat crist wrott on . wíth his honde.   to Moses;

And tok þe lawe . to Moyses.

320   His folk to kepen . in godes pes.

¶ þe ȝerde of AAron . þat was good.   IV. Aaron's rod;

Hit turned watur . in-to blod.

And from blod . to water a-ȝen

324   To schewe . þat þei weore gode men.

¶ Angel mete . men seiþ þer is.   V. Angels' food (Manna);

And of the bones . and þe fisch.   VI. Parts of the[?] Loaves and Fishes

þat crist fedde . fiue þousend men.   that fed 5000 men, and of the

328   And Relef lafte . aftur hem.²   Fragments; VII. Christ's

¶ þer beoþ cloþes . of Ihesu crist.   clothes; VIII. John the

And askes . of seint Ion þe Babtist.   Baptist's ashes; IX. The table-

And þe cloþ . þat crist gon wiþ him lede   cloth of the Last

332   On scherþorsday . his disciples wíth to fede.   Supper;

¶ ³ And þe cloþ . þat crist was wounden Inne   X. Christ's swad-

Whon he was child . for monnes sinne.³   dling cloth;

¶ Of Blod . and Watur . þer is also.   XI. Blood and Water from

336   þat out of cristes sydes . gan go.⁴   Christ's side;

¶ And of his Flesch . þat circumcise   XII. Christ's fore-

Men hit holden . in gret a prise.⁵   skin, &c., &c.

And oþer Relikes moni on.

340   In worschupe of crist . and seint Ion.

Here mai we . no lengore be.

In to þe popes halle . moste we.   In the *Pope's Hall*

In þat halle . þre dores þer be.   are three doors;

344   Vche day open . ȝe may hem se

---

¹⁻¹ Omitted by C.—see l. 388—not by L.

² C. transposes this and the line above, and inserts after it l.
400-15, about the four Pillars of Brass, and St John's Chains.

³ C. alters these; see l. 426-7.   ⁴ C. inserts l. 424-5.

⁵ C. inserts l. 430-7.

passing through
them gives

As often as þou passest . þorw eny of hem.

And entrest . þorw a-noþer þen.

And passest þorw a-noþer . of hem þre.

40 years' pardon. 348 Fourti 3er . is graunted to þe.[1]

In *Sancta Sanc-
torum* is a figure

Nou passe we . to *sancta sanctorum.*

þat is þe Chapel . of Clericor*um.*[2]

of the Saviour þer Inne is . þe saluatour.

352 To whom men doþ . gret honour.

sent to Our Lady
from heaven

þe whuche was sent . to vre ladi.

Whon heo was . in eorþe vs bi.

by Christ; From hire sone . þat is a-boue.

356 After þe tyme . of his Assencione.[3]

and the heads of
Peter and Paul

¶ Of Peter . and Poul . heore hedes ben þere.

Wel I.-closed . vnder þe hei3e Autere.

And oþer Relikes . mony on.

locked in a stone, 360 þer ben closed in a ston.

of which the
Pope keeps the
keys.

¶ Hose is þer . pope of Rome

þe keyes w*ith* him . he haþ I.-nome

þat no mon may hem þer I.-seo.

364 Bot he him self . present beo.

Full remission is
to be had there.

In þat chapel . 3if þou wolt craue

Plener remissiou*n* . þou mai3t haue.

At *Holy Rood
Church* is a Chapel

At þe chirche . of þe holy Roode.

368 Is a chapel . feir and gode.[4]

that Constance
built.

Constance . þat holi wommon.

Of kyng Constantyn . heo com.

His dou3ter heo was . and þat is scene.

372 For þorw preyer . of seynt Elene. .

þat holy place . heo made þus.

In þe honour . of þat holy crois.

Silvester granted Pope Siluestre . hit halewed þo

376 And gret pardou*n* . he 3af þer-to

---

[1] C. inserts l. 448—461.

[2] C. has 'In þat chapelle shall*e* no womon come,' l. 463, p. 130.

[3] C. alters the next eight lines; see l. 470-6, p. 130.

[4] C. inserts l. 480-1, p. 130-1.

Vche Sonenday . in þe ȝer.

And Wednesday . ȝif þou beo þer.

Of pardoun two hundred . and fifti [1] ȝer.

380 And cueri day . an hundred is þer.

And a sponge of galle . and Eysel.

Of þat venym . is þer gret del.[2]

þat Jewes profred him . to drinke þo

384 Whon he seide . Ciscio.

And a nayl . whon Crist Ihesu was.

Don on Rode tre . for vre trespas.

¶ In þat Chirche . is also

388 Of þe Croys . he was on do.

þat heng on Rode . him by.[3]

And of his sunnes . hedde Merci.

And a Titil . of sire pilat.

392 þei may hit rede . þat beo þerat.

þis is Ihesu . of Nazareth.

Kyng of Iewes . þat þolede deth.

þat titel is hud . hit wol not ley.

396 In A Croys . þat hongeþ hey.

In þe Maner . of a bouwe.

In mideward þe chirche rof .I. trouwe.

In þat maner . hit is do.

400 For no mon schulde come þer to.

Of more pardoun .I. wol ȝou say.

At seint Laurence . vche a day.

Seuen þousend ȝer . with lentons þer-to.

404 And þridde part . of þi penaunce vndo.

Pope pelagius . þat holy mon.

þat chirche . halewen he bi-gon.

And graunted al þat pardoun.

408 And þer-to . his Benisoun.[4]

Marginal notes:

It 250 years' pardon every Sunday and Wednesday,

and 100 every other day. Its Relics are— I. The Sponge of Gall and Vinegar offered to Christ on the Cross;

II. A nail he was crucified with;

III. A piece of the Penitent Thief's Cross;

IV. Pilate's Writing, "This is Jesus the King of the Jews."

At St Lawrence's daily is 7000 years' pardon, &c.,

---

[1] C. two thousand and fyfe.

[2] C. substitutes ' Relykes þer be mony & fele,' l. 494, p. 131, for this, and puts it before l. 401 here.

[3] C. makes it Christ's cross and the Thief's : l. 501-3, p. 132.

[4] C. inserts l. 522-31, p. 132-3.

and, for a year of Wednesdays, power to free a soul from Purgatory.

And ȝif þow be pere . al þe ȝer.

Vche Wednesday . in þat munster.

þenne hastou . of crist pouweer.

412 A. soule to drawe . from purgatori fer.

At *St Simplicius' Faustine* and *Beatrice*

At seint symple faustin . and beatris.

þat were verray Martirs . of pris.

Seint symple . pope of Rome he was.

416 God him sente . a wel feir gras.

are 7000 holy bones,

Vij þousende [1] holy bones.

He gedered to-gedere . but not at ones.

In his chirche . he dude hem graue.

420 He was siker . heore soules to saue.

and all men shriven there get

And ȝaf pardoun . to alle þo.

þat ben schriuen . and þider wol go.

7000 years' pardon and more.

Seue [2] þousend ȝer of pardoun . and more.

424 In þe honour of hem . þat liggen þore.[3]

Whon he was ded . þer was he graue

Crist his soule . mote saue.

At *St Vivian's*

At þe chirche . of seynt veuian.

428 Hit is writen . on a ston.

are 3000 martyrs buried,

þat þre þousend Martirs ben bured þare.

Crist leue here soules . wel to fare.

Honorius . þat holy pope.

432 þat chirche he halewed . in his cope.

and the pardon is 7000 years.

Seue þousend ȝer . of pardoun.

He ȝaf . [4] at þat processyoun.

To laste for euere more.[4]

436 To hem þat come þore.

¶ In þat churche . is an holy prest.

þat deore is . wiþ Ihesu Crist.

At *St Eusebius's*

Eusebius . was his name

440 To tellen of him . hit is no blame

---

[1] C. Seuen hondred, l. 540.   [2] C. Fyfe.

[3] C. omits the two next lines, and puts Iulyan for veuian, in l. 447.

[4-4] C. omits, and ends at l. 456 here ; l. 553, p. 134, *Pol., Rel., & Love Poems.*

Hit is writen . in a ston.

I. wol ȝou telle . or ȝe gon.

Pope Gregori . þer he dude stonde

444 Þe churche he halewed . wíth his honde.

And ȝaf pardoun . as I. ow say.

An hundred ȝer . and fifti day.

And þreo ȝer more .I. ow telle.

448 Forte Abate . þe peynes of helle.

At þe chirche . þer seint Iulian lith.

Þer is his chin . wíth his teth.

And oþer Relikes . mony and dere

452 To hem is graunted . Eiȝte þousend ȝere

A noþur chirche . ȝit þer is.

Of seint Matheu . men seyn hit is.

In þe wei . as þou schalt gon.

456 To þe Churche . of seint Ion.

Þer is an holy Arm . wel I.-diht.

Of seint Cristofre . Godes kniht.

In þat chirche . hit is do.

460 And gret pardoun . is graunted þer to.

For crist him selue þer-onne stod.

Whon Cristofre him bar . ouer þe flod.

Þer is a þousend ȝer . wíthouten mo.

464 And as mony lentones þer to.

IN þe Churche . of Viti . and Modesti

Þer mowe ȝe sitte and resti.

Þer is for-ȝeuen . þe þridde part of þi sinne

468 What tyme þou comest . þe chirche wíth-inne

Seue þousend Martirs . ben buried þere

As hit is writen . in þat Munstere.

In tyme of þe Emperour . Antony.

472 Hit is writen þer apertely[1].

IN þe Churche . of seint Anton[1]

Is seueþe part . þi penaunce vndon.

Is 100 years and
50 days' pardon,

and 3 years more
to abate hell's
pains.

At *St Julian's*

Is 8000 years'
pardon.

At St Matthew's

(where St Christopher's arm is,
. that Christ stood

on) is 1000 years'
pardon, &c.

At *St Vitus and
Modestus*

a third of your
sins are forgiven,

7000 Martyrs are
buried there.

At *St Anthony's*,
one-seventh of
your penance
excused.

[1] For these lines L. has one, l. 589, 'that tyrant was, and paynyme.'

At *St Mary the Major*

At seinte Marie . þe maiour.

476 þer is a chirche . of gret honour.

At þe heiȝe Auter . hit is seid.

lie St Matthew

þat þe bodi of seint Matheu . is leid.

and St Jerome,

And the bodi . of seint Jerom[1].

480 An holy doctor . he was on[1].

From þe Cite . of Damas.

He was brouȝt . in to þat plas.

before a chapel called Presepe (boards from the Manger of the Nativity).

Bi-foren a chapel . he was pit.

484 Presepe . men clepeþ hit.

Vppon his graue . lith a ston.

And a Crois . is graue þer on.

Aboue þe ston . a gredyl is.

488 Of Iren strong .I. wot hit is.

Its Relics are—

And Relikes þer ben . mony one[2].

In honur . of vr ladi . and hire sone[2].

I. The Cloth Christ was put in when He was born;

¶ A luytel cloþ . þer is þer-to.

492 In whuche cristes bodi . was furst in i-do

Of his Moder . whon he was born

To saue þe world . þat was for-lorn[3].

II. The Hay He lay on before the Ass;

¶ And of þat heiȝ . more and lasse.

496 þat crist lay on . bi-fore þe Asse.

III. An Arm of St Thomas a Becket;

¶ And an Arm . men seyn is þer.

Of seint Thomas þe holy Marter.

IV. Part of his brain;

And a parti of þe brayn.

500 At Canterburi . he was slayn.

V. His Rochet;

¶ And a Rochet þat is good.

Al be-spreint . with his blod.

Wheche he hedde on . whon he was take.

504 For al holi churche sake.

VI. An Image of Our Lady,

¶ And an ymage . sikerly.

Wonder feir . of vre ladi.

[1,1] L. varies; see l. 595-6, p. 135.

[2,2] For these lines L. has l. 605-8, p. 136.

[3] L. inserts l. 613-14 (about Christ's foreskin).

¶ Seint Luik . while he lyuede in londe.

508 Wolde haue peynted hit . wiþ his honde

And whon he hedde . ordeyned so.

Alle colours . þat schulde þer to.

He fond an ymage . al a-pert.

512 Non such þer was . middelert.

Mad wiþ Angel hond . and not wiþ his.

As men in Rome . witnesseþ þis.

And writen hit is al þere

516 On a table . atte heiȝe Autere

Pardoun þer is . þat men may se.

Graunted of popes . þat þer han be.

Vppon eueri chirche haly day

520 A þousend ȝer . þer haue þou may.

And þer to . þou schalt haue more.

Forȝiuenesse . of al þi sore.[1]

And eiȝte[2] hundred ȝer þer to.

524 Wel is him . þat þider may go.

In eueri feste . of vre ladi.

þerto graunted . seint Gregori.

An hundred ȝer . to pardoun.

528 And þerto godes Benysoun.

¶ In vre lauedi . þe Assumpcion,

þenne is þere . gret pardoun.

In to þe day . þat heo[3] was born.

532 Neuer a day . schal beo for-lorn.

In þat tyme . þer is fourtene þousend ȝer.

To alle þat come . to þat Munster.

A Chirche . ȝit þer is.

536 Prudencian . clepet hit is.[4]

For-ȝiuenesse . of al þi synne

At þat place . þer may þou winne.

Seint Gregori . telleþ þus.

540 In þat place . and in þat hous.

Marginal glosses (right column):

which St. Luke meant to have painted,

but one done by Angels' hands was put in its place.

On every Church Holy Day is 1000 years' pardon,

forgiveness of sorrows, and 800 years' more pardon.

At every Feast of Our Lady

100 years' pardon.

From the Assumption of the Virgin

to her Birthday

is 14000 years' pardon.

At St Prudencian's

---

[1] Altered in L. l. 624, p. 137.   [2] vii L.   [3] L. tylle Ihesu.

[4] L. inserts l. 657-8, p. 137 here, alters the two next lines, and adds two, l. 661-2, about St Preselle's churchyard, after them.

[Fol. 315 b. col. 1.]
are buried
4000 people:

and for every

body mentioned
by

pilgrims, they
get 1000 years'
pardon.

At *St Praxed's*

1300 martyrs

are buried.

Pope Innocent

granted every
man
1000 years'
pardon, &c.

At *St Martin's in
the Mount*

He Popes Sil-
vester and Leo,

and 800 saints,

800 years' pardon.

At *St Saviour's*

1000 years'
pardon.

Ben buried þer .I. vnderstonde.

Fourti [1] þousend . of diuerse londe.

For eueri bodi . þow wolt of spelle

544 Hit is writen . as I. ow telle.

þorw preyere of hem . þat þer be.

þis pardoun . is graunted to þe

For Peter and poul . þat sum tyme were

548 Boþe þei weoren . hostelled þere

þerfore alle pilgrimes . þat come þore.[2]

Hem is graunted a þousend ʒer . to hele her sore.[2]

At seint praxede . þat holy wommon.

552 riht þe soþe . tellen I. con.

A þousend bodies . with-outen mo.

And þreo hundred . ʒit þerto.

In þat place . buried þei be.

556 Heore soules with god . in dignite

þer suffrede deþ . in his tyme.

Emperour . seint Antonine.

Pope Innocent . after þan.

560 þer be graunted . to eueri man.

A þousend ʒer [3] . to pardoun.

And þridde part . þi sinnes remissioun.

‘At seint Martin . in þe mount.

564 þer stont a chirche . is not round.

Vnder þe heie Auter . liþ seluester . and . leone

þat weore popes . boþe in Rome

With oþere seyntes . monye I.-fere

568 Eiʒte hundred at ones . and as fele ʒere.

In þat wei . a Chirche þer is.

Of seint Saluatur .I. wot hit is.

Whon þou comest þer . þou maiʒt haue

572 A þousend ʒer . ʒif þou wolt craue

---

[1] L. *thre*, and alters the two next lines.

[2] L. omits these lines, but inserts l. 673-84, on *Titulus Pastoris*.

[3] L. 'O yere and xl dayes.'

[4] For the ten next lines L. has l. 697—702, p. 138.

A Nother day in þe 3er.

Of Seint peter . þe holy Marter.

A vincula . in þat londe

576 Lammasse day .I. vnderstonde.[1]

For in þat day . is gret pardoun.

For þer is plener . remissioun.

And eueri day . 3if þou wolt craue

580 Fyfe hundred 3er . þer mai3t þou haue

And as mony lentones mo

Pope gelasius . 3af þer to.

[2] þe Cheynes þere . men may se.

584 Sikerliche .I. telle þe

þer peter was bounden . sikerly.

While he was . in eorþe vs by.

To a noþer . moste we go.

588 þere Apostles . liggen two

Crist vs kepe alle from wo

preyeþ alle . þat hit beo so.[3]

Furst with Costantyn . hit was set.

592 And siþen with heretykes . doun I.-bet

Pelagius . and pope Ion.

þei duden hit maken vp anon.

And 3af þer to . pardoun gret.

596 To alle þat þider comeþ . be stret.[4]

For þer is . mony a noble seinte

þer þei liggen . and not beon peynte[3]

¶ Seint Jacob . and seint philip liþ in schrine

600 And mony a noþer[5] . holy virgine

And seint Sabyne . writen we fynde

And a Tabart . of seint Thomas of Inde[6]

Two þousend 3er . þer may þou haue

604 þi soule hit mai . from helle saue

On the day of St
Peter ad
Vincula ;

(Lammas Day,)

is full remission,

and 500 years'
pardon,
and Lents.

The Church of
The Holy
Apostles

was first built by
Constantine.

Many Saints lie
there :

St James,
St Philip, and

St Sabyne ; also
St Thomas's
Tabard.

The pardon is
2000 years,

---

[1] L. inserts l. 707-8, p. 139.

[2] For the next five lines L. has l. 715-23, on the Relics.

[3] L. omits this line.　　　　[4] L. omits these lines.

[5] L. Sent Eugenie þe.　　　[6] L. inserts l. 736-7, p. 139.

And vche day . whon þou comest þare.
þou maiȝt deliuere . a soule from care.

And on vche apostles . day.

608 þis pardoun is doubled . as I. ow say.

¹**A** þousend ȝer . þou maiȝt telle
At þe chirche . of seint Marcelle
þat was sum tyme . pope of Rome

612 For holi chirche . he soffrede Martirdome.¹

At seinte Marie . þe Rounde
þer stont a chirche . on þe grounde
þer is writen . as I. ow say.

616 þat . at . þe pretteneþe day . of may.²
At al halewe day . whon hit i-come²

þer is plener . Remissione³

A.-Grippa . dude hit make.

620 For Sibyl . and Neptanes . sake.

Modres þei weren of corsede men.

False fendes . ladden heom.

He ȝaf hit name . panteon.

624 In al Rome . was such non.

A vigour he made . of gold rede.
More þen God . he dude hit drede.
Whon hit . in þe temple sat.

628 Hit loked forþ . as a Cat.

He called hit Neptan . aftur his a-vys.
He lecuede þer on . he was not wys⁴

Vppon his heued . a couert of Bras.

632 To seynte petres . blowen hit was.
With a wynt of helle . as I. trouwe
For no mon mihte hit . þider haue þrowe.
þer hit stont I. telle þe.

---

¹⁻¹ L. has l. 742-5, p. 140, about St. Bartholomew's, given l. 711-12, p. 22, here.
² L. alters these lines.   ³ L. inserts 752-3.
⁴ L. puts l. 649 before l. 648, and inserts two (l. 766-7, p. 140) after the latter.

636 ȝif þou go þider . þou may hit se.[1]   and there you may see it.

ÞAt holy pope . Bonefas.   Pope Boniface

Was folfuld . of Godes gras[2]

To þe Emperour . soone he cam.

640 Julius . A wel good man.   asked the Emperor Julian for the Pantheon,

þat Temple he seide . þou ȝeue hit me

I. preye hit þe . for Charite.[3]

I. ȝeue hit þe . he seide . for euermore   got it,

644 In Amendement . of my sore.

þe Furste day . of Nouembre.   and on November 1

Pope Bonefas . with herte tendre.

þe folk of Rome . he gan to calle

648 And made hem semble . in þat halle

He gedered hem to-gedere . alle in-same

For þei wolde chaunge . þe halles name   changed its name to

In þe honour . of vre ladi.

652 And alle þe seintes . þat sit hire bi.

[4]þis halle schal hette . seinte Mari rounde   St Mary the Round.

He chaunged þe nome . in þat stounde

At seint Eustas . lihþ a good kniht.   At St Eustace's,

656 Placidas . sum tyme he heiht.   Placidas, his wife, and sons, lie.

He and his wif . and his twei sones I-fere

liggen buried . vnder þe heiȝe Autere.

Vche day . two þousend ȝer.   Pardon daily, 2000 years.

660 Pope Siluestre graunted þer.

[5]**A**t seint saluatour . is writen openly.   At St Salvadore, 1030 years' pardon.

A. þousend ȝer . and þritti[5].

At seint Celcy . is an hundred ȝer.   At St Cecilia's is a foot of Mary Magdalene.

664 A. fot of Marie Magdaleyn . is þer[6].

---

[1] L. inserts l. 773-4, p. 140-1.   [2] L. inserts l. 778-9, p. 141.

[3] L. inserts l. 784-5, and alters the two next lines here.

[4] L. alters the two next lines, and inserts l. 798, &c., here, and gives St Eustace's, altered at l. 850-55, p. 143. What follows l. 810 L., is represented here by l. 685-8, p. 22.

[5-5] L. has l. 856-63, p. 143.

[6] L. has first, l. 832-3, p. 142, and secondly, l. 861-7, p. 143.

At *St Mary Transpontine,* 800 years' pardon.

[1] And þre hundred ȝer . atte chirche faste bi.
þe nome is seint Marie transpedi.
þer is þe pilor þat peter *and* poul . was to bounde
668 And scourget . a swiþo gret stounde[1]

At *San Spirito,*

[2] **A**t þe chirche . of seynt spirit.
In þe weie . to trismere ful riht.

daily, 800 years' pardon.

Vche dai þer is . eiȝte hundred ȝer to pardoun
672 And þridde part of þi sunnes . remissioun[2].

At *St Mary Trastevere*

[3] At seinte Mario In trismere . þat ilke niht.
þat crist was boren . most of miht.
Sprong oyle . of a welle
676 As I. herde clerkes . in Rome telle

daily 2000 years' pardon.

Vche day . two þousend ȝer.
Of pardoun þou may haue þer[3].

At *St Gregory's* 300 years.
At *St Grisogono's* 400 years.
At *St Tyre and St John's* 800 years' pardon, &c.

At seint Gregories chirche þre hundred ȝer.[4]
680 And at seint grisogoni . four hundred is þer.[7]
In þe chirche of seint tyre . and seint Ion.[7]
þer is Eiȝte hundred ȝer . to pardon.
And þridde part of þi sunnes . Remission.
684 To alle men . þat þider wol cum.
þat graunted þere . pope vrban.
To alle þat þere . þider cam.
þat weoren out of dedly synne.
688 þat pardon þere . may he wynne.

At *St Lawrence's*

At seint laurence in Damas.[5]

500 years.

At *St Bartholomew's* 2000 years.

fyf hundred ȝer . is in þat plas.
At seint bartelmeuȝ . þat holi Marter.[6]
692 þer is of pardoun . two þousend ȝer.

At *St Angelo's*

[7] At seint Angel . as I. þe say

[1-1] L. gives this, altered, at l. 810-17, p. 141-2.
[2-2] L. gives this, altered, at L 818-21, p. 141. The Vernon MS. omits the L. St James, l. 822-5.
[3-3] L. gives this, altered at l. 826-31, p. 142.
[4] See L. l. 874-5, p. 143.   [5] L. l. 878-81, p. 143.
[6] L. l. 742-5, p. 140.   [7-7] New. Not in L.

A þousend ȝer . þer haue þou may.

Graunted of holi fadres . her bi-forn.

696 To saue soules . þat weore for-lorn[7].

[1]At seint Marie rochel ȝif þou wolt craue

two þousend ȝer . þer may þou haue[1].

[2] At seint petres prisoun.

700 Two þousend ȝer . of pardoun[2].

And an hundred ȝer . at seint Adrian[7].

[3] And as monye . at Cosma and Damian[3].

A þousend ȝer . at seint Marie þe newe verrement,[4]

704 And two þounsend ȝer . at seint Clement[8].

A M[L.] ȝer at seint Steuene certeynly [8].

And at seint Andreuȝes . ȝeres þritti[5].

[6] At seint saluatour . to pardoun . M[l.] ȝer.

708 Vche day in Bethleem . is granted þer.

Of Popus . þat þer han bene

To alle Men . þat ben clene

And to þat place . doþ eny good dede

712 He schal hit haue . to his mede.

[7]At seint Alexto . ȝif þou wolt gon.

þer þou maiȝt haue . to pardon.

Elleuene hundred ȝere

716 Vche day . þou maiȝt haue þere.

[8]At a Chapel . of vre ladi.

þer held scole seint Thomas of Canturburi.

viij .C. ȝer . is graunted þore.

720 And at seint vrbans chirche . iiij þousend more.

Eueriche day . to pardoun.

And þridde part . þi sinnes remission.

And ȝit þer is . more ouere.

724 þre hundred ȝere . foure score and and foure.

1-1 L. l. 882-91, p. 144. 2-2 L. l. 834-41, p. 142.
3 L. l. 848-9, p. 143. 4 L. l. 842-3, p. 142.
5 L. l. 896-906, p. 144. 6 L. l. 856-63, and see l. 3 above here.
7 L. l. 844-7, p. 142-3. 8-8 New. Not in L.

þat p*ar*dou*n* . popes þer han graunt.

To hem þat ben verrey repentaunt[s].

So much pardon
is there in Rome

[1]**I**N Rome . is muche p*ar*doun more

728 þen I. haue told . here bifore

that I can't tell it.

Or telle schulde . wiþ al my miht.

þouh I. weore her . boþe day . and niht.

God grant us some
of it,

Nou God . þat was . in Bedlem bore.

732 To saue þe world . þat was for-lore.

Graun*t* vs p*ar*t . of þis p*ar*doun.

and His blessing !

And þ*er* to . his Benisoun . Amen.

---

[1] The end is slightly altered in L. l. 907-14, p. 144.

INDEX OF NAMES AND CHURCHES.

[The references preceded by **C.** refer to the Cotton Text, by **L.** to the Lambeth Text, as printed in *Political, Religious, and Love Poems*, E. E. T. Soc., 1866, 113—144. The other References are to this Vernon Text.]

Aaron, the rod of, p. 11, l. 321 ; **C.** p. 127, l. 392.

Adrian's, St, p. 23, l. 701.

Agrippa, p. 20, l. 619 ; **L.** p. 140, l. 754.

Alexto's, St, p. 23, l. 713 ; **L.** p. 142, l. 844.

Alisaundre, Pope, p. 2, l. 27 ; **C.** p. 114, l. 35 ; p. 6, l. 173 ; **C.** p. 121, l. 224.

Altars, the 7 chief at St Peter's, p. 2, l. 35 ; **C.** p. 115, l. 51.

Amas, St, **L.** p. 117, l. 111, note 1.

Ambrose's, St, **L.** p. 143, l. 875.

Ananias, p. 3, l. 79 ; **C.** p. 117, l. 111.

Anastace's, St, p. 4, l. 94 ; **C.** p. 117, l. 130 ; **L.** p. 131, top note.

Andrew, St, altar of, p. 2, l. 41.

Andrew's, St, p. 23, l. 706 ; **L.** p. 144, l. 896.

Angelo's, St, p. 22, l. 693. *

Annes, St, **L.** p. 118, note 3.

Anthony's, St, p. 15, l. 473.

Anthonyne, Emperor, **L.** p. 135, l. 588 ; p. 15, l. 471 ; p. 18, l. 558.

Apostles, Church of, p. 19, l. 588; **L.** p. 139, l. 724.

Assumption-Day, **C.** p. 115, l. 75 ; p. 17, l. 529 ; **L.** p. 137, l. 649.

Austin's, St, p. 143, l. 875.

Bartholomew's, St, **L.** p. 140, l. 742 ; p. 22, l. 691.

Bastian's, St, p. 5, l. 147 ; **L.** p. 119, note 7 ; **C.** p. 120, l. 199.

Beatris's, St, p. 14, l. 413 ; **C.** p. 133, l. 536.

Benett, Pope, **L.** p. 119, note 7.

Bethlehem, p. 23, l. 708 ; p. 24, l. 731.

Blase, St, arm of, **L.** p. 139, l. 736.

Bonefas, Pope, p. 8, l. 231 ; p. 10, l. 285 ; **C.** p. 125, l. 348 ; p. 21, l. 637, 646 ; **L.** p. 141, l. 775, 789.

bones, 7000 holy, p. 14, l. 417.

brass, four Pillars of, from Jerusalem, **C.** p. 127, l. 408.

Cecilia's, St, p. 21, l. 663 ; **L.** p. 142, l. 832.

Cesar the martyr, **L.** p. 131, top note.

Chapels, 10,005 in Rome, **C.** p. 113, l. 20.

Urban, Pope, p. 4, l. 99 ; **L.** p. 134, note 1.

Urban's, St, p. 23, l. 720.

Vernicle, Altar of, p. 2, l. 37 ; pardon when V. showed, p. 3, l. 59 ; **C.** p. 116, l. 81 ; **C.** p. 128, l. 435.

Vevian's, St, p. 14, l. 427 ; **L.** p. 134, note 3.

Virgin Mary, second Chapel of, p. 5, l. 120-1 ; two chapels of, **C.** p. 118, l. 161 ; p. 5, **L** 140 ;

day of her Assumption, **C.** p. 115, l. 75 ; her milk, **C.** p. 128, l. 424 ; her image, p. 16, l. 505 ; **L.** p. 136, **L** 625 ; her chapel where Thomas à Becket kept school, p. 23, l. 717.

Vitus's, St, p. 15, l. 465 ; **L.** p. 135, **L** 582.

Wells, the Three, from St Paul's blood, p. 4, l. 113 ; **C.** p. 118, l. 153.

St Kateryne, p. 10, l. 291 ; Polit., Rel., and Love Poems, p. 125, l. 352. The *Saturday Review* of Dec. 22, 1866, p. 765, col. 1, suggests that this is " no doubt St Katharine on Mount Sinai, mentioned along with Jerusalem as an alternative point within the Holy Land." The *Penny Cyclopædia* says, " In the midst of the [Sinai] hills, on the height of Jebel Musa, surrounded by higher mountain-tops, and near the summit considered as the proper Sinai of Scripture, is situated the convent of St Catherine, founded, according to the credited tradition, by Helena, the mother of Constantine, in the fourth century." The most approved Legend, says Mr Morton, makes her sister to Constantine (p. xi., Pref. to " The Legend of St Katherine of Alexandria," Abbotsford Club, 1841). The Virgin is said to have married this Saint to Jesus Christ ; Maxentius (by some writers), or Maximinius (by others), is said to have tortured her, and put her to death. No contemporary writer mentions her (Morton, p. xi.).

[From Mrs Ormsby Gore's Porkington MS. No. 10, fol. 132, ab. 1460-70 A.D.]

IN rome bethe ij^C paresche churchs, & vij & x ^C chapell*is* and v. The Cytty his about þ° wallys xlij myllys, and ou*er* them byn ij ^C & lx tourr*is.*

In þ° Cetty byn xiiij prynssepall*e* gatt*is.* ¶ Be-fore þ° mynst*ur* of sent pett*ur* ys A steyre of xxviij grecys. Pope Alysaundu*re* granttyd vij ʒere of pardoñ at eue*r*y grece as hofte as anny mañ gothe hem w*i*tt ¹ good dewocyon; & aboufe þ° grece-ys ys a chappell*e* alon*e*, þat sent*e* pett*ur* sanng*e* in his furst mase. There ys vij M¹ ʒere of pardon, & so many lentt*is*, as oft as hit ys veset*e* w*i*tt devosyoñ. ¶ In þ° mynst*ur* byn a C autorr*is*, & at eue*r*y aut*ur* ys xxviij ʒere of pardon, and so mony lentt*is* grau*n*t at þ° havllowyng*e* by þ° sayde pope. ² But vij byn moche & most of dygnyte, þat is to say, furst on þ° ryʒtt hond ys þ° aut*ur* of þ° varnacull*e*. ¶ The ij of þ° honour*e* of our*e* lady : The þred of sent symon & Iude : The iiij of cent androw : The v of sent grego*r*ye, and þer he lythe : The vj of sent leoo þ° pope : The vij of þ° holly cros, & þer*i*n commythe no woman. And Eue*r*y aut*ur* ys eue*r*y day vij ^C ʒere, & so mony lentt*is*, of pardoñ. ¶ And at þ° hy haut*ur* ys fore-ʒcyfnys of synnys þat he fore-

St Peter's.
There are 100
steps,

[¹ MS. w*i*tt *all*
through]

and 100 altars,

[² Fol. 132 b.]
whereof 7 are
Chief Altars,

at each of which
is great pardon,
but more at the
High Altar.

gettyn, & fowys¹, & xxviij ȝerc of pardon granttyde of   [¹ ? MS. ? =faults]
gregory þᵉ pope: from holly-roode daye to lammas ys
euery day xiiij Mˡ ȝere of pardon. ¶ Oñ our lady   On the Assumption of Our Lady,
day þᵉ somsyon ys a Mˡ [ȝ]ere of pardoñ ¶ On sent   1000 years'
pettur and paullis day ys ij Mˡ ȝer of pardoñ   ¶ On   pardon.
sent marttayn þᵉ vij day was þat place hallowyd. Then
ys xxviij Mˡ ȝcre of pardoñ, & so mony lenttis, &
þᵉ þrede part & of pennance vndo ¶ When they   Of the Pardon when the Ver-
schowe þᵉ warnakoll, ys iiij Mˡ ȝere of pardon ; to   nicle is shown.
pepule of oþer placys ix Mˡ ; & ȝefe he pase þᵉ see
xiiij Mˡ, & þᵉ þredc part of synnys fore-²geyve ¶   [² Fol. 133.]
And in Lent euery pardoñ ys dovbullyd³ ¶ And þer   [³ ll crossed, as for e]
byñ holly bonnys of seynt pettur, & poulle,³ & symond,   Bones of Sts Peter, Paul,
& iude, gregorye, lyoñ, pernell, & oþer mo : þᵉ pardoñ   Pernelle, &c.
can no mañ tell þat þer is ¶ Frow sent pettur vn-to
poulles is iiij myle : to þat pardouñ þe pardoun fulle   St Paul's.
gret ¶ And in þᵉ conuercyoun of paulle is ij Mˡ
ȝere, & in his daye I Mˡ ȝcre, & at chyldormas day in
crystynmas ij Mˡ ȝcre. On sent mertayn þᵉ Xiij day
þat mynsteyre was hallowyd : Then ys xxviij Mˡ
ȝcre of pardoun, & þᵉ þrede part of pennance vndo ; & he
þat is þer euery sondaye in þᵉ ȝcre haþe as moche par-
don as ȝeyf he went to sent lamis ¶ Frow sent   [³ ll crossed, as for e]
paullis³ to sente austens is ij myle of feyre waye : þer is   St Austin's.
euery day viij Mˡ ȝere of pardoun, & þᵉ þred part of
paynance vndo, granttyd by pope vrban ; & sylvester
grant for-geyfnis of wrathe-þinge of fadore & modore, so
he layde no vyolent honde on hem ¶ Be-fore þᵉ dore   The Stone that St Paul's head
ys þᵉ ston þat sent paullis hede lay on ; & þer be iij   lay on.
wellis³ of gret vertu ¶ And þer ys ⁴A chappelle þat   [⁴ Fol. 133 b.]
men calle schalla cely, þat ys of oure lady, & fele holly   Schalla Cely.
bonnys byñ vndur þᵉ autur, x Mˡ merturis in þᵉ tyme
of tybure-rya þᵉ emparoure. he þat saythe a mase þer   A mass said there brings a soul
witt good devossyoñ may brynge a soule out of pul-   from Purgatory.
catorry to heyvyñ, & gretly helpe his frende þat is
alyue . & iij Mˡ ȝcre of pardon ys granttyde by popys

[¹ MS. *faded*]

Our Lady the Annunciate.

St Fabian's and Bastian's.

[² Fol. 134.]

The Martyr-Popes' Chapel

under-ground.

St John Lateran.

The Emperor Constantine converted by Silvester.

[³ Fol. 134 b.]

Christ's Table, and Moses's Tables of stone.

St Saviour's.
[⁴ MS. senatoure.]

xlvij þat liue at sent sebestyañdc¹. Conformyde be vrbanc, scluester, bennet, leoñ, & clement ¶ Frowe sent austens to oure lady þᵉ anuncyat ys ij loñge myle : þer ys v C ȝcre of pardoñ. A meraculle of oure lady was þer schewyde ¶ Fro sent maryc anuncyant to fabyan & bestyan þcr aperyd a nangelle to señt gregory at þᵉ hyȝhe autur at mase, & sayde þer was reymyssioñ granttyde of godc, xl M¹ ȝcre of pardoñ ; & so mony lenttis pope pallagyus ȝaffe þerto ¶ There lay pettur & paulo ij C ȝcre ore they wcre fonde : þer is more pardon þcn is at señt petturis ȝefc of dyueris popis, for þat place is havllowyd witt þᵉ bonnis ²of monny scynttis. A lyttylle be sydc ys a chappelle, & þcr lyne xxviij popis marturis, & þer is playñ reymyssioñ, & hc þat dyithe þᵉder-warde schall be sawyde fore his good entent. ¶ Thus chappell ys vnder þᵉ ground, & men most go to hit witt candyl lyȝtc ; fore sum tyme men þat wer holly, hyde þem þerin to do gret pennaunce fore þᵉ love of godc ¶ Frowe fabyañ & bestyañ to sent Iohñ þᵉ lattron: þer is pardoñ granttyd be þᵉ prayere of sent Iohñ þᵉ vangelyst, þer is not more pardoñ in alle rome, & be þᵉ preyere of sent Iohñ þᵉ Babtysto ¶ The Emparoure Costantyñ was conuertyd by pope· sylvestur; he ȝaufe hym his palles to make hit. þᵉ hous of godc, & þᵉ holly pope syluestur ȝaufe þerto pardon to hem þat is cleyne confessyde, & reypentaunce of his synne, & vesettythe þat place devotly ; as cleyn as þᵉ soulc parttythe frow þᵉ flesche, so cleyn hc be of alle his synnys ; & as scnt bonyface wytnyssythc, hc þat wyll truly fette pardoun, ³they nedythe not to go to þᵉ holly land. ¶ There is þᵉ tabulle þat cryst madc on his maunday, & ij tabulleis þat hc made witt his one hond, & wrōt his lawis þat hc toke to moysses ; & þᵉ clothis of señ Iohñ, & þᵉ scherte þat cryst weriyde, þat oure lady mad ; & þᵉ syrcumsysc of crystys flesche. ¶ There ys a chappell of sent scuatoure⁴ : cuery day

ix M¹ ӡere of pardoñ ys at þat place ¶ There ys a
saluatur þat was sent to oure lady froo heyvyñ. And
sent syluestur clossyd þᵉ¹ heddis of pettur & poull in   [¹ MS. þe þe] ⁚
þᵉ hy autur on sent Iohñnys day yᵉ ӡere of ouré lorde a
M¹ CCC & iij ӡere, & hit fell oñ a þorsday, & in þᵉ rofe
ouer þᵉ popys seo ys a fayre saluatur þat neuer vas
peynt witt mans honde ¶ And at þᵉ chappell of þᵉ holly   *Holy Rood Chapel.*
rood ys euery sonday & wennisday ij C. & 1 ӡere, &
euery daye a C ӡere to pardoñ ¶ At sent lavrence ys   *St Lawrence's.*
euery day vij M¹ ӡere of pardoñ, & so mony lenttis, &
fore-ӡeyfnys of pennance vndo : & who-so be euery
Wennnysday þer in þᵉ ӡere, he hathe þᵉ grace of gode to
²be in cleyn lyue . þat place hallowyd sent gregorye   [² Fol. 135.]
¶ At sent Benyan þat lythe [neer] sent gellyañ, þer is   *St Benyan's. (Vivian's ?)*
a C ӡere of pardoñ ¶ At sent vytte & modesce ys for-   *St Vitus and Modestus's.*
geyfnys of þᵉ iiij part of youre synnys ¶ At sent   *St Antony's.*
antony ys fore-ӡefnys of þᵉ viij parte of synnys. ¶ At
sent praxsede þᵉ iiij parte of synnys ys fore-geyf ¶   *St Praxed's.*
At sent mary þᵉ maioure, at þᵉ hy autur ys þᵉ body of   *St Mary the Greater.*
sent maþewe & Ierone þᵉ holly doctur, & a nare of sent
Thomas þᵉ merttur, & his breyñ, & a rocket þat was   Thomas à Becket's relics.
spronge witt his blod þat he werryd at his takynge, &
of þᵉ hey þat cryst lay in be-fore þᵉ asse : & þer is a
ymage of oure lady, of angellis werke ¶ At sent
prudencian byn hyriud v M¹ marturis . þer is fore-
geyfnys of þᵉ iij parte of synne, & fore euery body of
þem is a C ӡere & xl dayis pardoñ ¶ At þᵉ mount of   *St Martin's Mount.*
sent marttayñ ys vij ᶜ ӡere to pardoñ ¶ At sent
pettur þᵉ ad vyncula euery day iij ᶜ ӡere to pardoñ, & at   *St Peter ad Vincula.*
lammas fulle reymyssyoñ ¶ At alle þᵉ paleis, at euery
apos³tyllys day ys iij M¹ ӡere of pardon ¶ At sent   [³ Fol. 136, back]
mary þᵉ rounde ys a churche vndure þᵉ vrthe ; & þer   *St Mary the Round.*
þᵉ xiiij day of may & alle haullowyn .day, is fulle rey-
missyoñ, & euery day I M¹ ӡere of pardon. ¶ At
sent austens lythe placydas þat was callyd, & nowe he   *St Austin's.*
ys sent Eusstas, & his wyfe, & his iij sonnys vndure

[¹ sent dotted out]

The Black Salvator.
St Cecilia's.
St Mary's in Trasponti.

þ°·hy aut*ur* ; pope pylag*ius* grauntlde iij M¹ ȝere of pardoñ ¶ At ¹ þ° blacke saluat*ur* be iij M¹ ij C & xl ȝere of pardoñ. ¶ At sent Celce ys I C ȝere of pardon : þer is a foott of mary mavdelen ¶ At sent mary in tr*a*sponti is ij C ȝere of pardoñ, Et C.

Explycyt tract*us* de indulgencia romana si*u*e apostolica. ·.

The Pilgrims Sea-Voyage.

(From the Trin. Coll., Cambridge, MS. R, 3, 19, t. Hen. VI.)

A SUPPLEMENT TO

"THE STACIONS OF ROME."

The Pilgrims Sea-Voyage and Sea-Sickness.

*From Trinity College Library MS. R, 3, 19, temp.
Hen. VI.*

Men may leue alle gamys,
That saylen to seynt Jamys !
Ffor many a man hit gramys[1],

4   When they begyn to sayle.

You leave all fun behind you when you sail to St James's !

Ffor when they haue take the see,
At Sandwyche, or at Wynchylsee.
At Brystow, or where that hit bee.

8   Theyr hertes begyn to fayle.

Directly you get on board

your heart fails,

Anone the mastyr commaundeth fast
To hys shyp-men in alle the hast,
To dresse hem sone about the mast,

12   Theyr takelyng to make.

the shipmen make ready,

With "howe ! hissa !" then they cry,
"What, howe, mate ! thow stondyst to ny,
Thy felow may nat hale the by ;"

16   Thus they begyn to crake[2].

hollow,

order you out of their way,

A boy or tweyñ Anone up styen,
And ouerthwart the sayle-yerde lyen ;—
"Y how ! taylia !" the remenaunt cryen,

20   And pulle with alle theyr myght.

and haul at the sails.

[1] A.S. *gram*, troublesome ; *gramian*, to anger.
[2] to boast, hector.

"Put the boat ready; our Pilgrims

"Bestowe[1] the boote, Bote-swayne, anoñ,

That our pylgryms may pley theron ;

will groan

For som ar lyke to cowgh and grone

ere night."   24   Or hit be full mydnyght.

"Haul up the bowline!

"Hale the bowelyne[2]! now, vere the shete[3]!—

Cooke, make redy anoon our mete,

Poor Pilgrims, can't eat!

Our pylgryms haue no lust to ete,

28   I pray god yeue hem rest !"

"Go to the helm ! what, howe ! no nere[4]?

Steward, a pot of beer!

Steward, felow ! A pot of bere !"

"Ye shalle have, sir, with good chere,

32   Anoñ alle of the best."

"Y howe ! trussa! hale in the brayles[5] !

Thow halyst nat, be god, thow fayles !

[1] I suppose that *Bestowe* has not here its present provincial meaning of *Stow away.*

[2] *Bowling,* or rather *Bow-line,* is a Rope made fast to the Leetch, or middle part of the out-side of a Sail, by two, three, or four other Ropes like a Crow's Foot, which is termed the *Bowling-bridle;* the use of it being to make the Sails stand sharp, or close, or by a Wind. *Sharp the main Bowlings, Hale up* or *set taught the Bowling,* are Sea-phrases us'd when the Bowling is to be pull'd up harder, or hal'd forwards on : And To *ease, cheek,* or *run up the Bowling,* is to let it out more slack. Phillips.

[3] To *Veer out a Rope,* is to put it out by Hand, or to let it run out of itself ; as *Veer more Cable, i.e.* let more of it run out · But this Word is not apply'd to any Running-Rope except the Sheats. *Sheats* (in a Ship) are Ropes bent to the Clews of the Sails, which serve in all the lower Sails to *hale aft* or *round off* the Clew of the Sail; but in the Top-Sails they are made use of to *hale home, i.e.* to draw close the Sail to the Yard-Arms (Those Planks under Water, which come along the *Run* of the Ship, and are clos'd to the Stern-post, are also call'd *Sheats*). To *Ease the Sheat,* is to *veer* it out, or to let it go out gently. To *Let fly the Sheat* is to let it run out violently, as far as it will go: so that the Sail will then hang loose, and hold no Wind. Phillips.

[4] no nearer, that is, don't go closer to the wind. G. M. Hantler.

[5] *Brails* (Sea-term), small Ropes put thro' Blocks, or Pulleys fasten'd on either side of the Ties, so that they come down before the Sails of a Ship ; their use being, when the Sail is furled across,

O se howe well*e* owre good shyp sayles !"   *How well she sails !*

36   And thus they say among.

"Hale in the wartake ¹!" "hit shal be done."   *Steward, lay the cloth ;*

"Steward ! couer the boorde anone,

And set bred and salt therone,   *give 'em bread and salt for dinner."*

40   And tary nat to long."

Then cometh oone and scyth, "be mery ;   *"Storm's coming."*

Ye shall haue a storme or a pery."

"Holde thow thy pese ! thow canst no whery,

44   Thow medlyst wondyr sore."

Thys mene whyle the pylgryms ly,   *The poor Pilgrims have their bowls by them, and cry out for hot Malmsey ;*

And haue theyr bowlys fast they*m* by,

And cry aftyr hote maluesy,

48   "Thow helpe for to restore,"

And som wold haue A saltyd tost,

Ffor they myght ete neyther sode ne rost ;   *they can neither eat boiled nor roast.*

A man myght sone pay for theyr cost,

52   As for oo day or twayne.

Som layde theyr bookys on theyr kne,

And rad so long they myght nat se ;—

"Allas ! myne hede wolle cleue on thre ! "   *"My head will split in three,"*

56   Thus scyth another certayne.   *says one.*

to hale up its Bunt that it may be the more readily taken up or let full. *Hale up the Brails*, or *Brail up the Sails*, an expression us'd by Sea-men when they would have the Sails hal'd up in order to be furled, or bound close to the Yard. Phillips.

¹ There is no such word in our modern sea-terms. If *war* is the *war* of *war*fare, *take* may mean tackle, and refer to some nettings or apparatus outside the vessel. But if, as is more probable, the *take* means *tack*, the rope running from the clew or corner of the lower square-sail, to fasten it inboard through a ring or the like in the deck—(the sheet runs also from the corner, but fastens the sail outside the bulwark, through which it runs to a cleat inside)—then *war* may mean left or right [? *guard*], according to the tack to be hauled in. The *bowline* runs from the perpendicular edge of the sail, a third down, to the mast in front, and pulls the sail against the wind so as to keep it bellied. G. M. Hantler.

The shipowner
comes

` `Then commeth owre owner lyke a lorde.

And speketh many A Royall worde,

to see that all's
right.

And dresseth hym to the hygh borde,

60   To see alle thyng be welle.

Anone he calleth a carpentere,

And byddyth hym bryng with hym hys gere,

The cabins are
made ready.

To make the cabans here and there,

64   With many a febylle celle ;

No sack of straw
even for you !

A sak of strawe were there ryght good,

Ffor som must lyg theym in theyr hood ;

I had as lefe be in the wood,

68   Without mete or drynk ;

For when that we shall go to bedde,

And the pump,
my goodness,
stinks enough to
kill you !

The pumpe was nygh oure beddes hede,

A man were as good to be dede

72   As smell therof the stynk !

EXPLICIT.

Clene Maydenhod.

(From the Vernon MS., ab. 1370 A.D., *in the Bodleian Library, Oxford.)*

A SUPPLEMENT TO

" H A L I   M E I D E N H A D ,"

(Early English Text Society, 1866.)

EDITED BY

FREDERICK J. FURNIVALL, M.A.,

TRIN. HALL, CAMBRIDGE.

LONDON:

PUBLISHED FOR THE EARLY ENGLISH TEXT SOCIETY,

BY N. TRÜBNER & CO., 60, PATERNOSTER ROW.

MDCCCLXVII.

Of Clene Maydenhod.

[Vernon MS. (ab. 1370 A.D.) fol. 299, col. 3 ; seventeen stanzas of eights. The stops are the metrical points and single-letter guards of the MS. The hyphens are the Editor's.]

Of clene Maydenhod.
To bo weddet clanly to god.

OF A trewe loue . clene *and* derne.
Ichaue I.-write þe A Ron.
How þou maiȝt . ȝif þow wolt lerne.

I tell you how
to love your
Love.

4　For to loue . þi lemmon.
þat trowest is . of alle berne.
And most of loue . chacche con.
Beo war . for he is sundel steorne.

8　His eȝe is euere . þe vppon.
・þou art wrouht . of such a kynde.
Wiþ-outen loue . maiȝt þou not be.
And neuer more . schalt þou fynde.

None is so sweet
and fair as He.

12　þat is so swete . and feir as he.
Ȝif þou miht hym . to þe bynde.
Wiþ trewe loue . bondes þre.
Wiþ al þin herte . wille . *and* mynde

16　From þe . wol he neuer fle
¶ Heddest þou founden . such a feere.
þat weore so feir . as Absolon.
And þer-to . so strong to tere

He is fairer
than Absolom,
stronger than
[Fol. 299 b. col. 1.]
Samson.

20　As in his tyme . was Sampson.

l. 1, derne; A.S. *dearn*, secret.
l. 2, Ron ; A.S. *run*, a letter, talk.　l. 6, chacche, ? catch, take.
l. 17, feere, mate, companion.　　　　l. 19, þer-to, also.

<table>
<tr><td>

richer and wiser
than Solomon.

Man's love is

fickle and false.

Man's love

is never constant;

blows off as leaf
on bough.
Put then away
man's love,

bind Christ in
thy heart.

He is meək,

lovely of face,
</td>
<td>

So Riche þer-to . þat he were.
And so wys . as Salomon.
I.-wis to him . riht nouȝt hit were.
24   þat þou hast chosen . to þi lemmon.
¶ For monnes loue . ȝif þou beo holde.
Hit lasteþ . but a luytel res.
And wiþ gyle . is al bi-folde.
28   Hit is Fikel . Fals and les.
Whon þou wenest . hit best to holde.
Hit wendeþ a-wey . as wyndes bles.
And bi-comeþ . wrest and colde.
32   For trewe loue . hit neuer nes.
¶ Loue þat wol not . wiþ þe a-byde.
And þou hit desyre . þou hast wouh.
Ar þou beo war . hit wol to-glyde.
36   Hit is fikel . Fals . and Frouȝ.
Hit is a-weyward . In vche [1] a syde
Whiles hit lasteþ . vnwrest *and* wouh.
Beo war . and seo . what wol be-tyde
40   Hit wol to-dryue . as lef on bouh.
¶ þe loue þat wole . to serwe wende.
þou do hit al . out of þi þouȝt.
And his loue . in þin herte bynde
44   þat haþ þi loue . so deore a-bouȝt.
For ȝif þou heddest . al to þe ende.
Heuene *and* corþe . þorwȝ-out souht.
To fynde a feere . þat weore so hende.
48   As he . I.-wys hit weore for nouȝt.
¶ He is of Mood . wel Meke and Mylde.
Freo of herte . strong of miht.
Of glade chere . of wordes vn-wylde.
52   Of louesum leore . and Eiȝen briht.
</td></tr>
</table>

[1] MS. adds in vch.

l. 26, res; A.S. *ræs*, course, race.   l. 28, les; A.S. *leas*,
counterfeit, loose.   l. 31, wrest ; ? A.S. *wræst*, delicate, gentle.
l. 36, Frouȝ, frough, loose, spongy, brittle. (Halliwell.)

3if þou wolt do þe . in his mylde
And him al-one . loue ariht.
With-Inne þin herte . wol he bylde
56 And wone wiþ þe . boþe day and niht.   *ever constant.*
¶ Wel more murþe . is in his steuen.
þen herte may þenke . or tonge neme.
As be þe swan . þe blake Rauen.
60 Also be him . þe sonne gleme.   *He is brighter than the sun;*
No more is no þing . to him I.-lyche.
þen Galle is . to þe hony streme.
Of him is al þe Ioye . of heuene-riche   *He is the joy of heaven.*
64 þat with his grace . alle þing wol leme.
¶ 3if Mon be ded . and he him Ryne.   *He raises the dead to life.*
He reiseþ him . to lyue anone
For wele *and* wynne . serwe and pyne.
68 Al is Buxom . to him one
3if þow him wole . in herte wel tyne.
And kepe þat he . not from þe gon
Holde him . wiþ loue lyne.   *Love's bonds alone hold Him.*
72 For oþer bond . holdeþ him non.
¶ Is non founden . here in londe.   *None is so rich as He:*
þat is so Riche Mon . of Fee
For more good . he haþ in honde.
76 þen herte may þenke . or ei3e mai se.
Nis kyng . kniht . sweyn . ne bonde.   *He is over all.*
þat heo to him . mote Boxum be
He haþ I.-send . a derne sonde
80 And desyreþ to haue þe loue of þe.   *He desires thy love;*
¶ He askeþ wiþ þe . nouþer lond ne leode.   *He asks no dower with thee ;*
Gold ne seluer . ne precious stone.
To such þinges . haþ he no neode
84 Al þat is good . is wiþ hym one

l. 53, mylde; A.S. *milde*, mercy, pity.
l. 58, neme; A.S. *nemnan*, name.   l. 64, leme; A.S. *leoman*,
enlighten.   l. 65, Ryne; A.S. *rynan*, whisper.
l. 67, wynne; A.S. *wyn*, pleasure.   l. 68, buxom; A.S. *buhsom*,
obedient.   l. 69, tyne; A.S. *tynan*, to hedge in, enclose.

He gives thee
Heaven,

paved with gold,

where no night is,

If thou wilt love
Him, Christ.
For this,

[Fol. 209 b. col. 2.]
keep thyself
chaste,

pure under
petticoat.

Nothing does
God love more
than Maiden-
hood,

which once lost,
can never be
found again.

All the gold of
Arabye

ȝif þou with him . þi lyf wolt lede
And graunte to ben . his owne lemmon.
I . wot ful wel . what worþ þi meede.
88 Forsoþe . þe heuene riche won.
¶ þe weyes ben alle . þere I.-bete.
Wiþ Riche gold . þat schyneþ briht.
þe Ioyful song . in vche a strete
92 þer is day . and neuer more niht.
To synge . wol þei neuer lete.
To worschupe god . with al heore miht.
þat Blisse forsoþe . schal be þe mete.
96 ȝif þou Ihesu crist . loue ariht.
¶ ȝif þou wolt . þi lemmon qweme.
And to his brihte boure be brouȝt.
In Chastite . kep þou þe clene.
100 þat þou ne be . I.-wemmed nouht.
Non hony Com . þat renneþ on streme
Was neuer ȝut . so swete wrouht.
Ne neuere so briht . sonne gleme.
104 þen Mayden . þat is clene of þouȝt.
¶ While þou art clene . vnder gore
Bi-fore God . þou art ful heiȝe
þer is no þing . he loueþ more
108 þen Maidenhod . to wonen him neiȝe
Ne lerne þou neuere . þat ilke lore
Wher þorw þou leose . Mayden Beiȝe.
þe þing þat mon . may fynde no more.[1]
112 Bot he hit kepe . he is vn-sleȝe.
¶ þauȝ al þe gold . of Arabye.
Riche Rynges . and ȝymmes stone.

[1] See the Burlesque Recipe to restore Maidenhood in *Reliquiæ
Antiquæ*, vol. i. p. 250-1, A.D. 1520

l. 87, worþ, shall be.·   l. 93, lete; A.S. *lætan*, leave.
l. 97, qweme; A.S. *cweman*, please.   l. 100, Iwemmed; A.S.
wem, a spot; *wemme*, stained. l. 110, Beiȝe; A.S. *beáh*, ring, crown.
l. 112, vnsleȝe, unsly, foolish.   l. 114, ȝymmes stone, gem
stones. See l. 121.

And all þe tresour . of Asye.

116 Of oþer londes . euerichone.

· Weore bi-taken . in þi Baylye

To welden and hauen . in þi wone

Hit neore nou3t . to þe drnwerie

120 Of clene Maidenhod . al one.

¶ Hose . þis 3eem ston miht.

Louken . in a swete loue ryng.

He schulde schyne . also briht.

124 As sonne doþ . wiþ-outen endyng.

And beo holden . a ful swete wiht.

Bi-fore god . [and] al Monkynde.

þat wolde . in a Mayden liht.

128 Ful swete hit is . of hire þe Muynde.

¶ Lord 3if us . miht and grace.

Chaste lyf . þat we ne spille.

Verrey compungeion . and space.

132 Repentaunce . of dedes ille

And 3if vs miht . to folwe þi trace.

Euer more . boþe loude and stille.

þat to þe siht . of þi swete face.

136 On domes day . we may come tille.

and Asye

are nothing worth by the side of Maidenhood.

Whoever preserves this

is held full sweet by Christ.

Lord, give us grace to live chaste lives,

and follow Thy footsteps!

---

l. 119, druwerie ; O. Fr. *druerie, drurie,* amitié, attachement, amour, passion ; de l' ahal (Old High German), *trât, drût,* aujourd' hui *traut,* dilectus. Burguy.

l. 121, hose, whoso. l. 128, Muynde ; A.S. *myne,* thought, memory.

Early English Poetry, Folk-lore, &c.

Speedily will be published. To be completed in 10 *Parts, price* 2s. 6d. *each, forming one thick* 8vo *volume, closely printed in double columns.*

A

HANDBOOK

TO THE

EARLY POPULAR, POETICAL, AND DRAMATIC LITERATURE OF · GREAT BRITAIN,

FROM THE INVENTION OF PRINTING TO 1660.

BY W. CAREW HAZLITT,

EDITOR OF "REMAINS OF THE EARLY POPULAR POETRY OF ENGLAND,"
&c. &c. &c.

*** This work, which has been an eight or nine years' labour of love to the Editor, will bring together in a convenient compass a large variety of fresh information, and very numerous notices of unknown or undescribed editions and works in Early English and Scotish Literature.

JOHN RUSSELL SMITH, SOHO SQUARE.
(BY WHOM SUBSCRIBERS' NAMES WILL BE RECEIVED.)

Early English Text Society.

Third Annual Report of the Committee. January, 1867.

ONCE more the Committee have the pleasing task of announcing to the Members the still continuing success of the Society. Since its first year its annual income has more than quadrupled (152*l*. to 681*l*.) ; its yearly issue of Texts has nearly trebled (4 to 11) ; its members have nearly trebled (145 to 409), and never before has any Society of a like kind, in any year, given to the public such a variety and amount of the records of early English thought and work. During the past year the Society's Texts of 1864 and 1865 have nearly all gone out of print ° ; and the Committee's order to the printers for future issues has consequently been raised, first from 500 to 750, and then from 750 to 1000 copies. Moreover, the past year has been signalised by the direct co-operation of two of the older Societies — the Philological and Camden — with our own in the production of certain of our Texts, and by the efforts of the Kent Archæological Association to circulate the Society's edition (Mr. Morris's) of the most important monument of the early Kentish dialect, *The Ayenbite of Inwyt.* Could this co-operation be carried further, each Society offering yearly to all the others with similar aims a share in such of its publications as those other Societies might severally choose, a great boon would be conferred on students ; each Society would lighten the cost of publication to its own members, and largely extend the circulation of the books it produced, and which it should wish to see in the hands of as many readers as possible.

° As future Subscribers are sure to want these back Texts, the Committee have opened a separate Reprinting Fund, to which, until all the Texts that need reprinting are reprinted, they will carry all subscriptions for 1864–5–6, as well as the amount received for reprinted Texts and for the Texts of 1866 now in hand. Mr. Wheatley will receive and enter the names of those present and future Members who will undertake to buy the Texts of any back year when reprinted ; and as soon as the number of promises reaches the amount required for reprinting the Texts of any one year, they will at once be sent to press, and issued to the Members subscribing for them. The Texts of 1864 will cost about 120*l*. to reprint (of which 30*l*. may be looked on as already provided), and the Texts of 1865 about 300*l*. If 200 fresh Members to take the back Texts can be obtained during this year, as they should be, the reprinted Texts of both 1864 and 1865 can be issued in 1867. No subscriptions for any current year will be carried to this Reprinting Fund, as the Committee will adhere to the plan which has alone enabled them to produce so many Texts as they have done, that of spending each year's subscriptions for the benefit of those who contribute them.

The Committee declare their intention of thus offering the Society's Texts to other Printing bodies, and appeal to them to do the like to the Early English Text Society.

Another most gratifying circumstance in the past year has been the marked success of the examinations at Universities and Colleges for the Society's prizes of two years' issues of its Texts*. The winners of these prizes were,—

Winners.	*Examiners.*
R. F. Rumsey, Brasenose.	
A. H. Sayce, Queen's.	Rev. Prof. Bosworth, Oxford.
F. C. Channing, Corpus.	
George F. Drapes.	Prof. Ingram, Trinity Coll., Dublin.
— Bayles.	„ Brewer, King's Coll., London.
J. D. Fitzgerald.	„ Morley, Univ. Coll., London.
Harold R. Hopwood.	„ Greenwood, Owen's Coll., Manchester.
Thomas Stewart Ormond.	„ Masson, Edinburgh.
J. M. Campbell.	„ Nichol, Glasgow.
John F. Ewing.	„ Baynes, St. Andrew's.
F. Lawrence Rentoul.	„ Craik (the late), Belfast.
L. P. O'Connor.	„ Moffett, Galway.
Michael Burke.	„ Rushton, Cork.

So far as the Committee can judge from the reports of the different Professors to them, and from the answers of some of the Students that have been sent up to them, they look on the stir which the Society has thus given to the study of our early Literature in so many centres of intellectual life as one that will produce the best results, especially now that the publication of Mr. R. Morris's *Early English Extracts* (in the Clarendon Press Series) puts, for the first time in the history of the language, a trustworthy text-book and guide into learners' hands. The generous way in which the Professors have responded to the Society's call, giving often extra lectures, and always extra examinations, for the Prizes, calls for special acknowledgment on our part. Already one School has followed the example of our Colleges. To the Rev. Edwin A. Abbott, Head-master of the City of London School, belongs the credit of having introduced *Piers Plowman* as a class-book for his highest form, and of having insisted on a thorough training in English throughout his School. This is the beginning, the Committee trust, of a general knowledge of English historically by Englishmen, and they have gladly added to their list of annual prize-receivers this City School.

Two other events the Committee also allude to with pleasure : 1. The publication of an accurate Text from the best MS. of each of Chaucer's Poetical Works by Mr. Richard Morris (though, unfortunately, without

* Though there are not now two years' issues in hand for next season's prizes, the number of 12 Texts given will be kept up.

the collation and notes that the editor desired to add); and, 2, The undertaking to edit Bishop Percy's long-hidden folio MS.—the foundation of his celebrated *Reliques*—by three members of the Society, Professor Child, Mr. Hales, and Mr. Furnivall. It was only the entire absorption of the Society's limited resources by works already in the press, and its consequent inability to meet a call for 600*l*. in six months, that prevented the manager of the Percy scheme from making it part of the Society's ordinary work, and the Committee from undertaking it. As it is, the print of the MS. will be obtainable by members of the Society at half the cost to non-members, and the Committee give notice that they will consider the Arthur and other Romances in the Percy folio as part of the Society's Texts, and as not needing reproduction in the Society's series to which such Romances, &c. belong. The completion by the Surtees Society of their edition of the text of the Lindisfarne and Rushworth Gospels is also matter of congratulation; and it is to be hoped that the Glossary to, and Treatise on, the dialect of these inestimable Northern remains, promised by their latest editor, will soon follow the works themselves. Lastly, the Committee call attention to the assignment by Mr. Henry Bradshaw, to BARBOUR, the author of *The Brus*, of two works hitherto unknown to be written by him : 1. Fragments of a Troy-Book, mixed up with some copies of Lydgate's Troy-Book ; and, 2, nearly 40,000 lines of *Lives of Saints*. Should no other Society print these before our own is ready to undertake them, they will be issued among the Early English Text Society's publications in due course. The Anglo-Saxon Book of Martyrs that Mr. Cockayne has just claimed as King Alfred's, is to be printed by that gentleman in his *Shrine*.

Turning now to the Society's special work—the issue of Texts—the Committee note that in its first class, Romances, during the last year four books have been issued, two of which are printed from unique MSS. for the first time : *Merlin*, Part II., *Kyng Horn*, part of *Floris and Blancheflour*, and *Partenay*. The *Gawaine* Poems were kept back by their editor's other engagements ; but they are now ready for press, and will be sent to it forthwith.

In the Society's second class—Dialectal works—the event of the year has been the issue of the first great monument of the Kentish dialect, in 1340 A.D., the *Ayenbite of Inwyt*, not mutilated, as in the former edition, but complete, and with an almost exhaustive glossary and a treatise on the dialect by Mr. Richard Morris. The same dialect has received further illustration from the early treatises edited by Mr. Cockayne, the latter of which—*Hali Meidenhad*—has also brought into bright relief a passage in the life of English girls in 1220–30 A.D., unequalled in interest by any known publication of the time. The Northern dialect has been illustrated not only by the continuation of the works of Schir David Lyndesay of the Mont, Lord Lyone Kyng of Armes, with his eloquent denunciation of the wrongs of his time, but by the first treatises of the Society's complete edition of Hampole's works, accompanied by the unique and much-desired Life of the

Hermit*, edited by Mr. Perry, whom we thank for thus re-creating for us this old English worthy.

Into the third, or Religious class of the Society's Texts, fall as well the Ayenbite, Seinte Marherete, Hali Meidenhad, and Hampole tracts, already alluded to, as the Assumption of the Virgin, edited by Mr. Lumby, and the Religious Poems, edited by Mr. Furnivall. By these the superstitions and faith of our forefathers have been illustrated ; and of one Poem, carefully annotated by Mr. Wm. Rossetti, *The Stacions of Rome*, a second, and earlier text—discovered after the issue of the first —will be published.

Though the fourth and Miscellaneous class received last year no such accession as the *Wright's Chaste Wife* brought to it in the year before, yet the printing of the Political Poems from the Lambeth MS. 306 has at least proved the wisdom of having gleaners after Government labourers in the field ; and *The Boke of Quintessence* has exhibited some of the oddities in the rise of that science which, as modern Chemistry, commands the admiration and respect of men. The *Piers Plowman* extracts have cleared the way for Mr. Skeat's complete edition of the poem, and are a guarantee to members and the public that all care will be used in securing the best texts, and in collating them with the others next in value.

On the whole, while the Committee look back with some satisfaction to the results of the past year, they cannot but feel how much more might have been effected if the generality of members had exerted themselves to procure new subscribers in the way that a few of their body have done. Among these, the Committee desire publicly to thank the Local Secretary in Manchester, Mr. John Leigh, who, although he had in the first half of the year obtained twelve new subscribers, on the issue of Mr. Furnivall's Circular in June promised at once to obtain twelve more subscribers: and did so. Our Publisher, too, has been very zealous in the Society's behalf; and his list numbers 33 subscribers. Now this is working for editors, as editors work for members; and when once this spirit animates the whole of our subscribers, a real beginning will be made to the work the Society has set itself—the bringing to light the whole of the hidden springs of the noble Literature that England calls its own. The Society's is the first resolute attempt at this colossal work, as a whole, and it rests simply in the hands of our members whether the work shall be done or not. The present year should see the Society's income of last year at least doubled, for the revenue from the sale of past years' Texts is now exhausted, and then the way will be clear†.

The Texts that *can* be produced this year, if funds enough are supplied, are no less than thirty-two in number. Of these, three have already left the press‡, and are issued to members with this Report.

* A revised impression of the *Vita et Legenda* will be issued to members forthwith.

† We want also Editors in Oxford and Edinburgh.

‡ Immediate payment of the present year's subscriptions is required, in

Seven more are in the press, and thirteen more are ready to go to press at less than a month's notice: so that the work is well forward. The whole list of thirty-two is as follows, and ·the subscriptions received will determine how many of them will ⁑ sent out within the year:—

The Stacions of Rome, and the Pilgrims' Sea-Voyage and Sea-Sickness, with Clene Maydenhod. Edited from the Vernon and Porkington MSS. &c. by F. J. Furnivall, Esq., M.A. 1s.

Hymns to the Virgin and Christ; the Parliament of Devils; and other Religious Poems. Edited from the Lambeth MS. 853, by F. J. Furnivall, Esq., M.A. 3s.

Dan Jon Gaytrigg's Sermon; The Abbaye of S. Spirit; Sayne Jon, and other pieces in the Northern Dialect. Edited from Robert of Thorntone's MS. (ab. 1460 A.D.) by the Rev. G. Perry, M.A. 2s.

Levins's Manipulus, 1570; the earliest Rhyming Dictionary. To be edited by Henry B. Wheatley, Esq. [In the Press.

Piers Plowman's Vision; the earliest Version from the earliest MS. Collated throughout with three other MSS. of the same (or earliest) type. To be edited by the Rev. W. W. Skeat, M.A. [In the Press.

Piers Plowman's Crede. To be edited from the MSS. by the Rev. W. W. Skeat, M.A.

Various Poems relating to Sir Gawaine. To be edited from the MSS. by R. Morris, Esq. [In the Press.

Mirk's Duties of a Parish Priest, in verse. To be edited for the first time from the MSS. in the British Museum and Bodleian Libraries (ab. 1420 A.D.) by E. Peacock, Esq. [In the Press.

The Babees Boke, the Children's Book, Urbanitatis, The Bokes of Norture of John Russell and Hugh Rhodes, the Bokes of Keruyng, Cortasye, and Demeanour, &c., with some French and Latin Poems on like subjects. To be edited from Harleian and other MSS. by F. J. Furnivall, Esq. M.A. [In the Press.

The Knight de la Tour Landry, 1372. A Father's Book for his Daughters. To be edited from the Harleian MS. 1764 by Thomas Wright, Esq. M.A., and Mr. William Rossiter. [In the Press.

Palladius on Husbondrio; the earliest English Poem on Husbandry. To be edited from the unique MS. in Colchester Castle (ab. 1425 A.D.) by the Rev. Barton Lodge, A.M. Part I. [In the Press.

Cursor Mundi, or Cursur o Worlde, in the Northern Dialect. To be edited from the MSS. in the British Museum and Trinity College, Cambridge, by Richard Morris, Esq. Part I. [Copied.

Merlin, Part III. To be edited by H. B. Wheatley, Esq. [Copied.

Sir David Lyndesay's Works, Part III. To be edited by F. Hall, Esq., D.C.L.

Mayster Jon Gardener, and other early pieces on Herbs, &c. To be edited from the MSS. by W. Aldis Wright, Esq., M.A. [Copied.

Early English Homilies (ab. 1220–30 A.D.) from unique MSS. in Lambeth and Trinity College, Cambridge, Libraries. To be edited by R. Morris, Esq. [Copied.

Catholicon Anglicum. An English-Latin Dictionary (A.D. 1480). To be edited from Lord Monson's MS. by H. B. Wheatley, Esq. [Copied.

Chaucer. The Household Accounts of Elizabeth, wife of Prince Lionel, in which Chaucer is mentioned; with the other Documents relating to the Poet. To be edited by E. A. Bond, Esq., Keeper of the MSS. in the British Museum.

order that the printers' bills for these Texts may be discharged; and the Committee again request each Member to direct his Banker to pay his subscription on every first of January to the Society's account, at the Regent Street Branch of the Union Bank.

English Guilds, their Statutes and Customs, with an Introduction and
    an Appendix of translated Statutes. To be edited from the MSS. 1389 A.D.,
    by Toulmin Smith, Esq.   *[Copied.*
Chaucer's Prose Works. To be edited from the MSS., with an Essay on the
    Dialect of Chaucer, by R. Morris, Esq.; and a Treatise on the Poet's
    Pronunciation, by Alexander J. Ellis, Esq., F.R.S.   *[Preparing.*
Poems on Manners and Morals in the Northern Dialect, from a unique MS.
    in the Cambridge University Library. To be edited by the Rev. J. R.
    Lumby, M.A.   *[Copied.*
The Alliterative Romance of the Destruction of Troy, translated from Joseph
    of Exeter. To be edited from the unique MS. in the Hunterian Museum,
    Glasgow, by the Rev. G. A. Panton.   *[Copied.*
The Lay-Folks Mass-Book, and other Poems. To be edited from a Royal MS.
    &c., by the Rev. Frederick Simmons.   *[Copied.*
Lives of St. Juliane and St. Katherine, and other early pieces before 1250 A.D.
    To be edited from the MSS. (with a translation) by the Rev. O. Cockayne,
    M.A.   *[Copied.*
The Romance of William and the Werwolf. To be edited from the unique
    MS. in King's Coll. Library, Cambridge, by the Rev. W. W. Skeat, M.A.
                                    [Ready for Press.
The Romance of Sir Generides in Ballad Metre, from the unique MS. in
    Trin. Col. Library, Cambridge. To be edited by W. Aldis Wright, Esq. M.A.
Cato, Great and Little, with Proverbs, &c., from the Vernon and other MSS.
    To be edited by Mr. Edmund Brock.   *[Copied.*
The Rewle of Saint Benet, in Anglo-Saxon and Early English, &c., also in
    Northern verse of the 15th century. To be edited from early MSS. and
    the Cotton MS. Vesp. A. xxv. by R. Morris, Esq.
An Old English Bestiary of ab. 1250 A.D. To be edited from an Arundel MS.
    by R. Morris, Esq.   *[Copied.*
The Harrowing of Hell. To be edited from MSS, in the Bodleian Library,
    &c., by R. F. Weymouth, Esq., M.A.   *[Copied.*
Hampole's Translation of, and Commentary on, the Psalms, from the Northern
    MSS. in Sidney Sussex Coll. Cambridge, and No. 10 in Eton College
    Library, &c.. To be edited by R. Morris, Esq.
Le Venery de Twety and of Mayster John Giffarde, and the Mayster of Game.
    From MSS. Cott. Vesp. B. xii., Harl. 5806, &c. To be edited by Alfred
    Sadler, Esq.

A glance at the List above will show what important and interesting contributions will be made to our Literature if only the first
twenty of these books can be produced this year: a new Romance, the
continuation of a second; the first collection of the Statutes of our
Guilds, and the fullest collection yet made of tracts on the Meals and
Manners of our early times, illustrating the social condition of our
ancestors; the duties of the Parish Priest; the labours of the Husband-
man; the work of the Gardener; the warnings of the Divine; a Father's
Counsel to his Daughters, enforced by quaintest tales; traces of
CHAUCER (with a discussion of his dialect and pronunciation); the rise
of our great *Piers Plowman;* the story of the World; — surely, these,
with much most valuable material for the historian of our language
(among it, evidence of a new stage in the development of our tongue),
are worth an effort to produce during the year; and each member
must settle with himself whether he will make it.

List of Texts for Publication in future years :—

I. ARTHUR AND OTHER ROMANCES.

The Romance of Arthour and Merlin. From the Auchinleck MS. (ab.
1320–30 A.D.), and the Lincoln's Inn and Douce MSS.
The History of the Saint Graal or Sank Ryal. By Henry Lonelich, Skynner
(ab. 1440 A.D.) To be re-edited from the unique MS. in the Library of
Corpus Christi Coll., Cambridge, by F. J. Furnivall, Esq., M.A.
Syr Thomas Maleor's Mort d'Arthur. To be edited from Caxton's edition
(8145 A.D.), with a new Preface, Notes, and a Glossary.
The Arthur Ballads.
The Romance of Sir Tristrem. To be edited from the Auchinleck MS.
The English Charlemagne Romances, from the Auchinleck MS., Lansd.
388, &c.
A Charlemagne Romance in Southern verse (ab. 1377 A.D.): from MS. Ash-
mole 33. To be edited by the Rev. J. Hoskyns Abrahall, M.A.
The Romance or Legend of Sir Ypotis. From the Vernon and other MSS.
[Copied.
The English Alexander Romances. Chevalere Assigne.
The Early English Version of the Gesta Romanorum. To be edited from the
MSS. in the British Museum and other Libraries.

II. DIALECTAL WORKS AND DICTIONARIES.

The Gospel of Nicodemus in the Northumbrian dialect, To be edited for the
first time from Harl. MS. 4196, &c., Cotton-Galba, E. ix., by R. Morris,'Esq.
Lives of Saints, in the Southern dialect. To be edited from the Harleian MS.
2277 (ab. 1305 A.D.), by R. Morris, Esq.
Barbour's Lives of Saints (in the Northern Dialect). From the MS. in the
Cambridge University Library.
A Series of Early English Dictionaries.
A little Dictionary for Children (W. de Worde), or a shorte Dictionarie for
yonge beginners (1554), by J. Withals. (The earliest edition, to be col-
lated with the succeeding editions.) To be edited by Joseph Payne, Esq.
Abcedarium Anglico-latinum, pro Tyrunculis, Richardo Hulœto exscriptore.
Londini, 1552. To be edited by Danby P. Fry, Esq.
An Alvearie, or Quadruple Dictionarie in Englishe, Latin, Greeke, and French,
by John Baret. (The edition of 1580 collated with that of 1573.)
Also, Latin-English,—
Horman's Vulgaria, 1519, 1530. To be edited by Toulmin Smith, Esq.

III. MISCELLANEOUS.

The two later and differing Versions of Piers Plowman, in separate editions.
To be edited from the MSS. by the Rev. W. W. Skeat, M.A. *[Preparing.*
Early English Poems from the Vernon MS. To be edited by F. J. Furnivall,
Esq., M.A. *[Part copied.*
The Rewle of the Moon, and other Poems illustrating Superstitions. To be
edited from MSS. by F. J. Furnivall, Esq., M.A. *[Part copied.*
Vegecius of Knyghthod and Chyualrie, from MSS. in the Bodleian and British
Museum. To be edited by Danby P. Fry, Esq. *[Copied.*
The Siege of Rouen. From Harl. MS. 2256, Egerton MS. 1995, Harl. 753,
Bodl. 124, &c.
Lydgate's Tragedies of Bochas, or Falles of Princes. From the fine Harleian
MS. 1766.
Lydgate and Burgh's Secreta Secretorum. From the Sloane MS. 2464.
Lydgate's Translation of Boethius, A.D. 1410; Pilgrim, 1426; Siege of Thebes,
1448–50, and other Poems.
Hugh Campden's Sidracke. From MS. Laud, o. 57; Harl. 4294, &c.
Occleve's Unprinted Works.
Occleve's De Regimine Principum, from Arundel MS. 38.

Gawain Douglas's Æneis. To be edited by F. Hall, Esq., D.C.L.
Barbour's Brus, to be edited from the MSS. by J. Peile, Esq., M.A., and the
Rev. W. W. Skeat, M.A. [*Preparing.*
Barbour's Troy-Book. The Fragments in the MSS. of the Cambridge
University Library, and the Douce Collection.
The Siege of Jerusalem, the Nightingale, and other Poems, from MS. Cot.
Calig. A. ii., Addit. MS. 10,036, &c.
Lauder's remaining Poems. To be edited by F. Hall, Esq., D.C.L.
Early Lawes and Ordinances of Warre. To be edited by the Rev. F. Simmons.
George Ashby's Active Policy of a Prince, from MS. mm. iv. 42, in Camb.
Univ. Library.
Peter Idle's Poems, from the MS. ee. iv. 37, in Camb. Univ. Library.
Adam Davie's Poems, from MS. Laud. I. 74, and Hale's MS. 150.
A Collection of Early Tracts on Grammar. To be edited (chiefly from MSS.
for the first time) by H. B. Wheatley, Esq. [*Part copied.*
Some of Francis Thynne's Works. To be edited from the MSS. by G. H.
Kingsley, Esq., M.D.
Froissart's Chronicles, translated out of Frenche into our maternall Englyshe
Tonge, by Johan Bourchier, Knight, Lord Bernors. To be edited by
Henry B. Wheatley, Esq.
Skelton's Translation of Diodorus Siculus, oute of freshe Latin, that is, of
Poggius Florentinus, containing six books. To be edited for the first
time from the unique MS. in the Library of Corpus Christi Coll., Cam-
bridge.
William Harrison's Description of England, from Holinshead.
The English Works of Sir Thomas More.

IV. BIBLICAL AND RELIGIOUS.

The Psalms called Schorham's. To be edited from the unique MS. (ab. 1340
A.D.) in the British Museum, by R. Morris, Esq. [*Copied.*
Roberd of Brunne's Handlyng Synne; a treatise on the sins, and sketches of
the manners, of English men and women in A.D. 1303. To be re-edited
from the MSS. in the British Museum and Bodleian Libraries, by F. J.
Furnivall, Esq., M.A.
Amon and Mardocheus, or Haman and Mordecai. From the Vernon MS.
The Old and New Testament in Verse. To be edited from the Vernon MS.
by R. Morris, Esq. [*Copied.*
The Stories of Lazarus, Susanna and the Elders, &c. From the Vernon MS.
To be edited by J. W. Hales, Esq., M.A. [*Copied.*
The History of Adam and Eve. From MS. Harl. 1704. Edited by S. W.
Kershaw, Esq.
Trevisa's Translation of Fitzralf's Sermon. From MS. Harl. 1900.
Medytacions of the Soper of our Lorde Ihesu, &c., perhaps by Robert of
Brunne. To be edited from the Harl. MS. 1701 (ab. 1360 A.D.), &c., by
F. J. Furnivall, Esq.
Hampole's remaining Works.
Guillaume de Deguilleville's Pilgrimage of the Sowle, translated. From MS.
Cott. Vitel. c. xiii.
Lydgate's Life of St. Edmund. From the presentation MS. to Henry VI.
Harl. 2278.
William of Nassyngton's Treatise on Sins, &c.
John de Taysteke's Poem on the Decalogue, 1357 A.D. From MS. Harl. 1022.

₊ *All Complaints as to the Non-delivery of Texts should be made
to the Publishers.*

The Committee invite offers of voluntary assistance from those who may
be willing to edit or copy Texts, or to lend them books for re-printing or for
re-reading with the original MSS.

LIST OF SUBSCRIBERS.

ABRAHALL, Rev. John Hoskyns, Combe, near Woodstock.
ADAM, A. Mercer, Esq., M.D., Boston, Lincolnshire.
ADAMS, Dr. Ernest, Anson Road, Victoria Park, Manchester.
ADAMS, G. E., Esq. (Rouge Dragon), Heralds' College, E.C.
ADDIS, John, Jun., Esq., Rustington, Littlehampton, Sussex.
AINSWORTH, Dr. R. F., Cliff Point, Lower Broughton, Manchester.
AKROYD, Edward, Esq., Bank Field, Halifax.
ALEXANDER, George Russell, Esq., Glasgow.
ALEXANDER, John, Esq., Dowanhill, Glasgow,
ALEXANDER, Walter, Esq., 29 St. Vincent Place, Glasgow.
ALLON, Rev. Henry, 10 St. Mary's Road, Canonbury, N.
AMERY, J. Sparke, Jun., Esq., Druid, near Ashburton, Devon.
AMHURST, Wm. A. Tyssen, Esq., Didlington Park, Brandon, Norfolk.
ANGUS, Rev. Joseph, D.D., Regent's Park College, N.W.
ARDASEER CURSETJEE, Esq.
ASHER & Co., Messrs., 13 Bedford Street, Covent Garden. W.C. (4 sets.)
ATHENÆUM CLUB, Waterloo Place, S.W.
ATKINSON, Rev. J. C., Danby Parsonage, Grosmont, York.
AUSTIN, Frederick Stephen, Esq., 39 Princess Street, Manchester.
AUSTIN, Stephen, Hertford.
BABINGTON, Rev. Professor Churchill, B.D., St. John's College, Cambridge.
BACKHOUSE, John H., Esq., Blackwell, Darlington.
BAIN, J., Esq., 1 Haymarket.
BAKER, Charles, Esq., 11 Sackville Street, W.
BANKS, W. S., Esq., Wakefield.
BARON, Rev. J., Rectory, Upton Scudamore, Warminster. Wilts.
BAYNES, THOS. S., Esq., 19 Queen Street, St. Andrew's, Fife.
BEARD, James, Esq., The Grange, Burnage Lane, near Manchester.
BELFAST, THE LIBRARY OF QUEEN'S COLLEGE.
BENECKE, Dr., Berlin.
BENTLY, Rev. T. R., 12 St. John Street, Manchester.
BESLY, Rev. Dr. John, The Vicarage, Long Benton, Newcastle-on-Tyne.
BICKERTON, G., Esq., 28 Torphichen Street, Edinburgh.
BIDDELL, Sidney, Esq., Farm-hill House, Stroud, Gloucestershire.
BIRMINGHAM LIBRARY, Union Street, Birmingham.
BIRMINGHAM FREE CENTRAL LIBRARY, Ratcliff Place, Birmingham.
BLACKMAN, Frederick, Esq., 4 York Road, S.
BLADON, James, Esq., Albion House, Pont y Pool.
BOHN, Henry G., Esq., York Street, Covent Garden, W.C.
BOILEAU, Sir John P., Bart., 20 Upper Brook Street, W.
BOSWORTH, Rev. Professor, D.D., 20 Beaumont Street, Oxford.
BOWMAN, Henry, Esq., Victoria Park, Manchester.
BRIDGMAN, W. D. J., Esq., D.C.L., Woolwich Common, S.E.
BRITTON, John James, Esq., 5 Park Road, Newcastle-on-Tyne.
BROTHERS, Alfred, Esq., St. Ann's Square, Manchester.
BUCHANAN, Dr. Robert, Prince's Street, Greenock.
BUCKLEY, Rev. Wm. Edw., Rectory, Middleton Cheney, Banbury.

BUTE, The Marquis of, Christ Church College, Oxford.
BUXTON, Charles, Esq., M.P., 7 Grosvenor Crescent, S.W.
CAMBRIDGE, CHRIST'S COLLEGE.
    „   TRINITY COLLEGE LIBRARY.
    „   TRINITY HALL LIBRARY.
CARLYLE, Dr., The Hill, Dumfries, N.B.
CHALMERS, James, Esq., Aberdeen.
CHALMERS, Richard, Esq., 1 Claremont Terrace, Glasgow.
CHAMBERLAIN, Professor J. H., Grange House, Birmingham.
CHAPPELL, William, Esq., Sunninghill, Staines.
CHEETHAM, Rev. S., King's College, London, W.C.
CHELTENHAM COLLEGE LIBRARY.
    „   PERMANENT LIBRARY, 18 Clarence Street, Cheltenham.
CHESTERTON, Miss E., 12 Kensington Palace Gardens, W.
CLARK, E. C., Esq., Trinity College, Cambridge.
CLARK, Rev. Samuel, The Vicarage, Bredwardine, Hereford.
COHEN, Arthur, Esq., 6 King's Bench Walk, Temple, E.C.
COLEBROOKE, Sir T. E., Bart., 37 South Street, Piccadilly.
COLERIDGE, Miss Edith, Hanwell Rectory, Middlesex.
COLERIDGE, J. Duke, Esq., Q.C., 1 Brick Court, Temple, E.C.
COMBE, Thomas, Esq., University Press, Oxford.
CONSTABLE, Archibald, Esq., 34 Royal Terrace, Edinburgh.
COSENS, Frederick, Esq, Larkbere Lodge, Clapham Park.
COWPER, Joseph Meadows, Esq., Davington, Faversham.
COXHEAD, Albert C., Esq., 47 Russell Square, W.C.
CRAIG, Rev. John S., Maryport, Cumberland.
CREWDSON, Thos. Dilworth, Esq., 8 Cecil Street, Greenheys, Manchester.
CROSTON, James, Esq., Waterloo Road, Cheetham, Manchester.
CROUCH, Walter, Junr., 20 Coborn Street, Bow.
CROWTHER, Joseph S., Esq., 22 Prince's Street, Manchester.
DALTON, J. N., Esq., 6 Green Street, Cambridge.
DANA, C. S., Esq., United States.
DAVIES, Rev. John, Walsoken Rectory, near Wisbeach.
DAVIES, Robert, Esq., The Mount, York.
DE LA RUE, Warren, Esq., 110 Bunhill Row, E.C.
DE LA RUE, W. Frederick, Esq., 110 Bunhill Row, E.C.
DEVONSHIRE, The Duke of, Devonshire House, Piccadilly.
DICKINSON, F. H., Esq., Kingweston House, Somerton, Somerset.
DODDS, Rev. James, The Abbey, Paisley, N.B.
DONALDSON, David, Esq., Grammar School, Paisley.
DONALDSON, Rev. John, Edinburgh.
D'ORSEY, Rev. A. J., B.D., 9 Upper Seymour Street West, Hyde Park, W.
DOWDEN, Edward, Esq., 8 Montenotte, Cork.
DOWSON, Alfred C., Esq., High Dock, Limehouse, E.
DRAKE, W. H., Esq., 2 Newton Terrace, Faversham.
DREW, Alfred, Esq., 2 Raymond Buildings, Gray's Inn, W.C.
DUBLIN, King's Inn Library, Henrietta Street.
    „   Right Rev. Richard C. Trench, Archbishop of, Dublin.
DURIEN, W. M., Esq., St. John's College, Cambridge.
EARLE, Rev. J., Swanswick Rectory, Bath.
EASTWICK, Edward B., Esq., 38 Thurloe Square, S.W.
EDINBURGH UNIVERSITY LIBRARY.
EISDELL, Miss S. L., Colchester.
ELLIS, A. J., Esq., 2 Western Villas, Colney Hatch Park, N.
ELT, C. H., Esq., 1 Noel Street, Islington.
EUING, William, Esq., 209 West George Street, Glasgow.
EVANS, Sebastian, Esq., 145 Highgate, near Birmingham.
EYTON, J. Walter K., Esq., 46 Portsdown Road, Maida Hill, W.
FAIRBAIRN, Rev. James, Edinburgh.
FERGUS, Dr., 30 Elmbank Street, Glasgow.
FIELD, Hamilton, Esq., New Park Road, Brixton Hill.

FITCH, J. G., Esq., Heworth House, York.
FLETCHER, John Shepherd, Esq., Lever Street, Piccadilly, Manchester.
FOARD, James T., Esq., 5 Essex Court, Temple, E.C.
FOGO, David T. Lawrie, Esq., 145 West George Street, Glasgow.
FORSTER, John, Esq., Palace-gate House, Kensington, W.
FREETHY, Mr. Frederick, Working Men's College, London.
FROGGATT, Thomas, Esq., Burnage Lane, near Manchester.
FRY, Danby P., Esq., Poor Law Board, Whitehall.
FRY, Frederick, Esq., Wellington Street, Islington.
FURNIVALL, F. J., Esq., 3 Old Square, Lincoln's Inn, W.C.
GEE, William, Esq., High Street, Boston.
GIBBS, Captain Charles, 2nd Regiment.
GIBBS, H. H., Esq., St. Dunstan's, Regent's Park.
GIBBS, William, Esq., Tyntesfield, near Bristol.
GILBERT, J. T., Esq., Royal Irish Academy, Dublin.
GILLETT, Rev. Edward, Runham Vicarage, Filby, Norwich, *Local Sec.*
GIRAUD, Francis F., Esq., South House, Faversham.
GLASGOW UNIVERSITY LIBRARY.
GLEN, W. Cunningham, Esq., Poor Law Board, Whitehall.
GLENNIE, J. Stuart, Esq., 6 Stone Buildings, Lincoln's Inn, W.C.
GOLDSTÜCKER, Professor, 14 St. George's Square, N.W.
GOLDTHORP, J. D., Esq., Wakefield.
GORDON, Rev. Robert, 14 Northumberland Street, Edinburgh.
GRAHAME, W. F., Esq., Madras Civil Service.
GREEN, Rev. Henry, Knutsford, Cheshire.
GREG, Louis, Esq., 9 Rumford Street, Liverpool, *Local Sec.*
GREG, Mrs. E. H., Quarry Bank, Wilmslow, Cheshire.
GREY, George, Esq., County Buildings, Glasgow.
GRIFFITH, Rev. H. T., North Walsham, Norfolk.
GRIFFITH, Robert W., Esq., Quay Street, Cardiff.
GROOME, Rev. Robert, Monk Soham Rectory, Wickham Market.
GUEST, Edwin, Esq., LL.D., Master of Caius College, Cambridge.
GUEST, John, Esq., Moorgate Grange, Rotherham.
GUILD, J. Wylie, Esq., Glasgow.
GUILDHALL, LIBRARY OF THE CORPORATION OF LONDON, E.C.
HAIGH, Rev. Dr., Bramham College, near Tadcaster.
HAINES, Frederick, Esq., 178 Prospect Place, Maida Hill East.
HALES, J. W. Esq., 7 Crown Office Row, E.C.
HALKETT, Samuel, Esq., Advocates' Library, Edinburgh.
HALL, B. H., Esq., Troy, New York.
HALL, Fitzedward, Esq., D.C.L., 18 Provost Road, Haverstock Hill, N.W.
HALLIWELL, J. O., Esq., 6 St. Mary's Place, West Brompton, S.W.
HAMILTON, Andrew, Esq., 47 Rumford Street, Manchester.
HAMLEN, Charles, Esq., 27 Virginia Street, Glasgow.
HANSON, Reginald, Esq., 37 Boundary Road, N.W.
HARRIS, William, Esq., Stratford Road, Camp Hill, Birmingham.
HARRISON, W., Esq., Galligreaves Hall, near Blackburn, Lancashire.
HART, Howard, Esq., Troy, New York.
HAYES, Francis B., Esq., United States.
HEALES, Alfred, Esq., Doctors' Commons, E.C.
HERFORD, Edward, Esq., The Knolls, Alderley Edge, near Manchester.
HERFORD, Rev. W. H., 33 Wood Street, Greenheys, Manchester.
HEWITT, Thomas, Esq., Bella Vista, Queen's Town, Cork Harbour.
HODGKIN, Mrs., West Derby, Liverpool.
HODGSON, Shadworth H., Esq., 45 Conduit Street, Regent Street, W.
HOETS, J. W. Van Rees, Esq., 150 Adelaide Road, N.W.
HOPKINS, Hugh, Bookseller, 6 Royal Bank Place, Glasgow.
HOPWOOD, J. R., Esq., Trinity College, Cambridge.
HORNBUCKLE, J. W., Esq., London Hospital.
HORWOOD, Alfred J., Esq., New Court, Middle Temple, E.C.
HOWARD, Hon. Richard E., D.C.L., Stamp Office, Manchester.

HUTCHINSON, Captain R. R., 13 Holland Terrace, Holland Road, Kensington.
HYDE, James John, Esq., 10 Lomas Buildings, Bull Lane, Stepney, E.
INDIA OFFICE LIBRARY, Cannon Row.
INGLEBY, C. Mansfield, Esq., LL.D., Valentines, Ilford, E.
JACKSON, E. Steane, Esq., Tettenhall Proprietary School, near Wolverhampton.
JACKSON, Rev. S., Magdalen College, Cambridge.
JEFFERY, Counsell, Esq., 30 Tredegar Square, Bow Road, E.
JENNER, Charles, Esq., Easter Duddingston Lodge, Edinburgh.
JOHNSON, Prof. G. J., 243 Hagley Road, Birmingham.
JOHNSON, S. G., Esq., Faversham.
JOHNSON, W., Esq., Eton College, Windsor.
JONES, C. W., Esq., Gateacre, near Liverpool.
JONES, J. Pryce, Esq., Grove Park School, Wrexham.
JONES, Thomas, Esq., Chetham Library, Manchester.
JORDAN, Joseph, Esq., Bridge Street, Manchester.
KERSHAW, John, Esq., Cross Gate, Audenshaw, Manchester.
KERSLEY, Rev. Canon, Ll.D., Middleton Vicarage, King's Lynn.
KETT, Rev. C. W., 17 St. George's Square, Regent's Park Road, N.W.
KING, W. Warwick, Esq., 29 Queen Street, Cannon Street West, E.C.
KITCHIN, Rev. G. W., Walton Manor, Oxford.
KITSON, James, Esq., Elmete Hall, Leeds.
LAING, David, Esq., Signet Library, Edinburgh.
LATHAM, Henry, Esq., 34 Beaumont Street, Oxford.
LECKIE, Thomas, Esq., M.D., 29 Upper Southwick Street, Hyde Park, W.
LEIGH, John, Esq., Whalley Road, Whalley Range, Manchester, *Local Sec.*
LIPPINCOTT, Messrs. J. B. & Co., Philadelphia (5 sets).
LODGE, Rev. Barton, Colchester.
LONDON LIBRARY, 12 St. James's Square, S.W.
LUARD, Rev. Henry Richards, 4 St. Peter's Terrace, Cambridge.
LUCK, Frederick George, Esq., West Farm, East Barnet, Herts.
LUCK, Michael George, Esq., Acre Wharf, Lambeth.
LUMBY, Rev. J. Rawson, St. Mary's Gate, Cambridge.
LUSHINGTON, E. L., Esq., Park House, Maidstone, and Glasgow.
MAC DONALD, George, Esq., 12 Earle's Terrace, Kensington, W.
MAC DOUALL, Professor Charles, LL.D., Queen's College, Belfast.
MACKENZIE, John Whitefoord, Esq., 16 Royal Circus, Edinburgh.
M'LAUGHLIN, Captain E., R.A., 28 Maryon Road, Charlton.
MACMILLAN, A., Esq., Bedford Street, Covent Garden, W.C.
MACMILLAN, Messrs., Cambridge.
MADDEN, Sir Frederick, K.H., 25 St. Stephen's Square.
MALLESON, William T., Esq., Duppa's Hill Common, Croydon.
MANCHESTER, The Duke of, Kimbolton Castle, St. Neot's.
MANCHESTER, The Lord Bishop of, Mauldreth Hall, near Manchester.
MARKBY, Rev. Thomas, Trinity Hall, Cambridge.
MARSH, His Excellency George P., Florence.
MARTINEAU, Russell, Esq., British Museum, W.C.
MAYOR, Rev. John E. B., St. John's College, Cambridge.
MEDLEY, Rev. J. B., Tormarton Rectory, Chipping Sodbury.
MEDLICOTT, W. G., Esq., Longmeadow, Massachusetts, U. S.
MELBOURNE PUBLIC LIBRARY, Victoria.
MELBOURNE UNIVERSITY, Victoria.
MONK, F. W., Esq, Faversham.
MONSON, The Lord, Burton Hall, Lincolnshire.
MORESHWAR, Mr., 3 St. George's Square, Primrose Hill, N.W.
MORRIS, Richard, Esq., 10 Stamford Road, Page Green, Tottenham.
MUIR, John, Esq., 16 Regent's Terrace, Edinburgh.
MÜLLER, Professor Max, 64 High Street, Oxford.
MUNBY, Arthur J., Esq., 6 Fig-tree Court, Temple, E.C.
MUNTZ, G., Esq., Albion Tube Works, Birmingham.
MURDOCH, James Barclay, Esq., 33 Lynedoch Street, Glasgow.
NAPIER, George W., Esq., Alderley Edge, near Manchester.

Nash, D. W., Esq., Ethnological Society, St. Martin's Place.
Neaves, Lord, 7 Charlotte Square, Edinburgh.
Newcastle-upon-Tyne, Literary and Philosophical Society.
Nichol, Professor, University, Glasgow.
Nichols, John Gough, Esq., 25 Parliament Street, Westminster.
Noble, Benjamin, Esq., 74 Union Street, Greenock.
Norfolk and Norwich Literary Institution, Norwich.
Norman, J. Manship, Esq., Dencombe, Crawley, Sussex.
Norris, Edwin, Esq., 6 Michael's Grove, Brompton, S.W.
Ogle, Messrs. Maurice & Co., Glasgow.
Owen's College Library, Manchester.
Paine, Cornelius, Jun., Esq., Oak Hill, Surbiton, Surrey.
Panton, Rev. G. A., Crown Circus, Dowanhill, Glasgow, *Local Sec.* (2 sets.)
Parker, H. T., Esq., 3 Ladbroke Gardens, W. (11 sets.)
Patterson, W. S., Esq., Glasgow.
Payne, Joseph, Esq., 4 Kildare Gardens, Bayswater, W.
Peace, Maskell Wm., Esq., Wigan, Lancashire.
Peacock, Edward, Esq., Bottesford Manor, Brigg, Lincolnshire.
Peacock, William, Esq., Sunniside, Sunderland.
Peel, George, Esq., Soho Iron Works, Manchester.
Peile, John, Esq., Christ's College, Cambridge.
Penfold, Hugh, Esq., Library Chambers, Middle Temple.
Penzance Public Library.
Perceval, Charles Spencer, Esq., 64 Eccleston Square, S.W.
Perry, Rev. George G., Waddington Rectory, Lincoln.
Picton, James A., Esq., Dale Street, Liverpool.
Pocock, Charles Innes, Esq., Hastings Terrace, Jersey.
Prange, F. G., Esq., 2 Grove Park, Lodge Lane, Liverpool.
Priaulx, Osw. De Beauvoir, Esq., 8 Cavendish Square, W.
Pritchard, James, Esq., Lendel Place, Paisley Road.
Putnam, G. Phelps, Esq., United States.
Quaritch, Mr., 15 Piccadilly, W.
Raine, Rev. James, York.
Ranken, Rev. W. A., Cuminestown, Turriff, N.B.
Reilly, Francis S., Esq., 22 Old Buildings, Lincoln's Inn, W.C.
Reynell, Charles W., Esq., 8 Hotham Villas, Putney.
Rivington, John, Esq., 12 Lower Seymour Street, W.
Roberts, Mr. Robert, Bookseller, Boston.
Rossetti, W. M., Esq., 166 Albany Street, N.W.
Royal Library, Windsor Castle.
Rumney, Robert, Esq., Ardwick Chemical Works, near Manchester. ·
Ruskin, John, Esq., Denmark Hill, Camberwell. (10 sets.)
Russell, Thomas, Esq., 14 India Street, Glasgow.
St. Andrew's University Library.
St. David's, Rt. Rev. Connop Thirlwall, Bp. of, Abergwili Palace, Carmarthen.
Salisbury, E. R. G., Esq., Glan Aber, Chester.
Schwabe, Edm. S., Esq., Oak End, Halliwell Lane, Chetham Hill, Manchester.
Schwabe, F. S. Esq., Rhodes House, Middleton, near Manchester.
Scott, James, Esq., The Lochies House, Burntisland, N.B.
Scott, William B., Esq., 33 Elgin Road, Kensington Park Road, W.
Shields, Thomas, Esq., Scarborough.
Simmons, Rev. Frederick, Dalton Holme, Beverley.
Sinclair, James B., Esq., 324 Dumbarton Road, Glasgow.
Sion College, President and Fellows of, London Wall, E.C.
Skeat, Rev. Walter W., 22 Regent's Street, Cambridge.
Slack, John, Esq., Croft Lodge, Rothesay.
Slatter, Rev. John, Streatley Vicarage, Reading.
Smith, Mr. Alexander, 214 New City Road, Glasgow.
Smith, Charles, Esq., Faversham.
Smith, Toulmin, Esq., Wood Lane, Highgate.
Snelgrove, Arthur G., Esq., London Hospital, S.

SNELL, Rev. W. M., Corpus Christi College, Cambridge.
SPARK, H. King, Esq., Greenbank, Darlington.
SPRANGE, A. D., Esq., 12 Princes Street, Bayswater, W.
STANLEY, The Lord, 23 St. James's Square, S.W.
STEPHENS, Professor George, University of Copenhagen, Denmark.
STEVENSON. Rev. Professor William, D.D., 37 Royal Terrace, Edinburgh,
STEWART, Alexander B., Esq., Glasgow.
STIRRUP, Mark, Esq., 62A Mosley Street, Manchester.
STOCKHOLM ROYAL LIBRARY.
STOKES, Whitley, Esq., Calcutta.
STORR, Rayner, Esq., Bariki House, Upper Norwood.
STRATHERN, Sheriff, County Buildings, Glasgow.
STUBBS, Rev. Professor W., Vicarage, Navestock, Essex.
SUNDERLAND SUBSCRIPTION LIBRARY.
SYMONDS, Rev. Henry, The Close, Norwich.
TAYLOR, Thos. F., Esq., Highfield House, Pemberton, near Wigan.
TENNYSON, Alfred, Esq., D.C.L., Faringford, Isle of Wight.
TEW, Rev. Edmund, Patching Rectory, near Arundel, Sussex.
THOMPSON, Frederic, Esq., Wakefield.
THORPE, Rev. J. F., Hernhill Vicarage, Faversham.
TIMMINS, Samuel, Esq., Elvetham Lodge, Edgbaston, Birmingham.
TOD, John, Esq., 11 Rumford Street, Liverpool.
TOOLE, The Very Rev. Canon, Bedford House, Hulme, Manchester.
TROLLOPE, T. A., Esq., Florence.
TROY, New York, Young Men's Association.
TRÜBNER & Co., Messrs. 60 Paternoster Row. (33 sets.)
TURNER, Robert S., Esq., 1 Park Square West, Regent's Park, N.W.
TYSSEN, John R. D., Esq., 9 Rock Gardens, Brighton.
VERNON, George V., Esq., Old Trafford, Manchester.
VIZARD, John, Esq., Dursley, Gloucestershire.
WAKEFIELD BOOK SOCIETY.
    „   MECHANICS' INSTITUTION.
WALES, George W., Esq., Boston, U.S.
WARD, Professor A. W., Owen's College, Manchester.
WARD, Harry, Esq., British Museum, W.C.
WATSON, Frederick Elwin, Esq., Mayor of Norwich, Surrey Street, Norwich.
WATSON, Robert Spence, Esq., Moss Croft, Gateshead-on-Tyne.
WATTS, Thomas, Esq., British Museum, W.C.
WEDGWOOD, Hensleigh, Esq., 1 Cumberland Place, Regent's Park.
WEYMOUTH, R. F., Esq., Portland Grammar School, Plymouth.
WHALLEY, J. T., Esq., 14 Marsden Street, Brown Street, Manchester.
WHEATLEY, Henry B., Esq., 53 Berners Street, W., *Hon. Sec.*
WHEELER, D. H., Esq., 17 Henrietta Street, Covent Garden, W.C.
WHITAKER, J. Esq., 10 Warwick Square.
WHITE, George H. Esq., 8 Bishopsgate Street within, E.C.
WHITE, Robert, Esq., 11 Claremont Place, Newcastle-on-Tyne.
WHITNEY, Henry Austin, Esq., United States.
WHITTARD, Rev. T. Middlemore, The College, Cheltenham.
WILBRAHAM, Henry, Esq., Chancery Office, Cross Street Chambers, Manchester.
WILKINSON, Dr. Alexander E., 10 Lever Street, Piccadilly, Manchester.
WILLIAMS, Sydney, Esq., 14 Henrietta Street, Covent Garden, W.C. (4 sets.)
WILLIAMSON, Rev. William, Rood House, Widcombe Hill, Bath.
WILSON, Edward J., Esq., 6 Whitefriar Gate, Hull.
WILSON, Lestock, P., Esq., 37 Wigmore Street, W.
WILSON, Richard M., Fountain Street, Manchester.
WILSON, Thomas, Esq., Crimbles House, Leeds.
WINWOOD, Rev. H. H., 4 Cavendish Crescent, Bath.
WREN, Walter, Esq., Wiltshire House, Brixton, S.
WRIGHT, W. Aldis, Esq., Trinity College, Cambridge.
WRIGHT, Thomas, Esq., 14 Sidney Street, Brompton, S.W.
YOUNG, Alexander, Esq., 138 Hope Street, Glasgow.

RECEIPTS.

	£	s.	d.
Balance at Bankers from Last Year's Account ...	50	5	1
Subscriptions:—			
1864. Sixty-eight at £1 1s. ...	71	8	0
Thirty-one (through Agents) at £1 ...	31	0	0
1865. Eighty-nine at £1 1s. ...	93	9	0
Thirty-four (through Agents) at £1 ...	34	0	0
1866. Two hundred and fifty-one at £1 1s. ...	263	11	0
Seventy-one (through Agents) at £1 ...	71	0	0
1867. Twenty-two at £1 1s. ...	23	2	0
1868. Two at £1 1s. ...	2	2	0
Sale of Texts ...	1	3	0
Philological Society (Share of Ayenbite of Inwyt) ...	40	0	0
	£681	**0**	**1**

PAYMENTS.

	£	s.	d.	£	s.	d.
Printing Account (Austin):—						
No.						
13. Seinte Marherete ...	4	8	9			
14. King Horn, &c. ...	43	18	9			
18. Hali Meidenhed ...	17	2	6			
21. Merlin ...	64	5	0			
Prospectuses, Stitching, Postages, Nos. 6, 7, 8, 9, &c. ...	16	17	0			
	146	6	9			
Less Discount ...	6	9	3	139	17	6
Ditto (Childs)						
No.						
15. Political, Religious, and Love Poems ...	81	12	5			
17. Piers Plowman ...	10	8	0			
19. Lyndesay's Monarche, Part II. ...	41	6	4			
22. Partenay ...	61	13	8			
23. Ayenbite of Inwyt ...	140	14	8			
3500 Copies of Report ...	14	7	4			
11,000 Prospectuses ...	7	8	6			
	377	5	8			
Less Discount ...	8	14	9	368	10	11
Ditto (Clarendon Press)						
No.						
16. Book of Quinte Essence ...	12	19	3			
20. Hampole's Treatises ...	29	7	11	42	7	2
Rev. O. Cockayne (for "Seinte Marherete") ...				20	0	0
Messrs. Asher (for various Nos. of 1864 and 1865) ...				2	13	0
Messrs. Trübner, &c. (for Delivery, Postages, &c.) ...				29	10	1
Petty Expenses:—						
Purchase of Books for re-editing ...				6	10	0
Copying Cursor Mundi, Vegeclus, Ayenbite, St. Juliano, &c. ...				30	8	3
Postages, Stationery, &c. ...				9	11	5
Commission on Country Drafts ...				0	1	9
Balance at Bankers ...				31	10	0
				£681	**0**	**1**

We have examined this Account with the Books and Vouchers, and certify that it is correct.

WM. CUNNINGHAM GLEN, } AUDITORS.
REGINALD HANSON, B.A., }

Early English Text Society.

The Subscription is £1 1s. a-year, due in advance on the 1st of January, and should be paid either to the Society's Account at the Union Bank of London, 14 Argyll Place, Regent Street, W., or by post-office order (made payable to the Chief Office, London) to the Hon. Secretary, Henry B. Wheatley, Esq., 53 Berners Street, London, W.

The Publications for 1864 and 1865 are out of print, but a few copies remain of No. 4,—Sir Gawayne and the Green Knight, ab. 1320-30, edited by R. Morris, Esq., 10s.; and No. 5, Of the Orthographie and Congruitie of the Britan Tongue, be Alexander Hume, ab. 1617 A.D., edited by Henry B. Wheatley, Esq., 4s. (No. 1 is Early English Alliterative Poems, ab. 1320-30 A.D.; 2, Arthur, ab. 1440 A.D.; 3, Lauder on the Dewtie of Kyngis, &c., 1556 A.D.; 6, Lancelot of the Laik, ab. 1500; 7, Genesis and Exodus, ab. 1250; 8, Morte Arthure, ab. 1440; 9, Thynne on Chaucer's Workes, ab. 1598; 10, Merlin, ab. 1450, Pt. I.; 11, Lyndesay's Monarche, &c. 1552, Pt. I.; 12, The Wright's Chaste Wife, ab. 1462.)

The Publications for 1866 (of which only a few copies remain) are—

13. SEINTE MARHERETE, þe Meiden ant Martyr. Three Texts of ab. A.D. 1200, 1310, 1330. First edited in 1862 by the Rev. Oswald Cockayne, M.A., and now re-issued. 2s.

14. THE ROMANCE OF KYNG HORN, FLORIS AND BLANCHEFLOUR, AND THE ASSUMPTION OF THE BLESSED VIRGIN. Edited from the MS. in the Library of the University of Cambridge by the Rev. J. Rawson Lumby, M.A. 3s. 6d.

15. POLITICAL, RELIGIOUS, AND LOVE POEMS, from the Lambeth MS. No. 306, and other MSS. Edited by F.J. Furnivall, Esq. M.A. 7s. 6d.

16. A TRETICE IN ENGLISCH breuely drawe out of þe Book of Quintis essencijs in Latyn, þat Hermys þe prophete and king of Egipt, after þe flood of Noe, fadir of Philosophris, hadde by reuelacioun of an aungil of God to him sente. Edited from the Sloane MS. 73, by F. J. Furnivall, Esq. M.A. 1s.

17. PARALLEL EXTRACTS FROM TWENTY-NINE MSS. OF PIERS PLOWMAN, with comments, and a Proposal for the Society's Three-text edition of the Poem. By the Rev. W. W. Skeat, M.A. 1s.

18. HALI MEIDENHAD, ab. 1200 A.D. Edited for the first time from the MS. (with a translation), by the Rev. Oswald Cockayne, M.A. 1s.

19. SIR DAVID LYNDESAY'S MONARCHE, Part II., the Complaynt of the King's Papingo, and other Minor Poems. Edited from the first editions by Fitzedward Hall, Esq. D.C.L. 3s. 6d.

20. SOME TREATISES BY RICHARD ROLLE DE HAMPOLE. Edited from Robert of Thorntone's MS. ab. 1440 A.D., by the Rev. G. Perry, M.A. 1s.

21. MERLIN, or the Early History of Arthur. Part II. Edited by Henry B. Wheatley, Esq. 4s.

22. THE ROMANCE OF PARTENAY OR LUSIGNAN. Edited for the first time from the unique MS. in the Library of Trinity College, Cambridge, by the Rev. W. W. Skeat, M.A. 6s.

23. DAN MICHEL'S AYENBITE OF INWYT, or Remorse of Conscience, in the Kentish dialect, 1340 A.D. Edited from the unique MS. in the British Museum by Richard Morris, Esq. 10s. 6d.

LONDON: TRÜBNER & CO., 60 PATERNOSTER ROW.
EDINBURGH: T. G. STEVENSON, 22 SOUTH FREDERICK STREET.
GLASGOW: OGLE & CO., 1 ROYAL EXCHANGE SQUARE.
BERLIN: ASHER & CO., UNTER DEN LINDEN, 20.
NEW YORK: C. SCRIBNER & CO.
PHILADELPHIA: J. B. LIPPINCOTT & CO.

Þ E S H R I N E,

A COLLECTION OF

OCCASIONAL PAPERS ON DRY SUBJECTS.

No. 1. Dr. Bosworth and his Saxon Dictionary.
  Life of St. Neot; from MS. Cott. Vesp. in Saxon
  English.

No. 2. Translation of Life of St. Neot.
  Postscript on Dr. Bosworths Dictionary.
  Latin of to day; a critique.
  Names of animals from a St. Gall MS.
  Yule week from a CCCC. MS. Saxon English.

No. 3 Is in þe press, and will contain Malchus, a story of
  Eastern adventure, in Saxon English, from a MS. in
  þe Cottonian Collection. And oðer matter.

 Each Number makes sixteen pages; and to Subscribers
the price is one shilling. Subscriptions received for past or
future Numbers by Oswald Cockayne, 17 Montague Street,
Russell Square, London. A volume of about 320 pages is
intended.

  Publishers: WILLIAMS AND NORGATE, London.

A DICTIONARY OF þE OLDEST ENGLISH,

VULGARLY MISNAMED ANGLO-SAXON,

From þe printed literature, and from a body of transcripts
of what remains unpublished, is in preparation by
OSWALD COCKAYNE, M.A. Cantab.

NARRATIVNCVLÆ.

Stories of Natural History in Saxon English from þe MSS.
Published by J. RUSSELL SMIÐ, London.

www.ingramcontent.com/pod-product-compliance
Lightning Source LLC
Chambersburg PA
CBHW031455270326
41930CB00007B/1017